What is *Post-Modernism*?

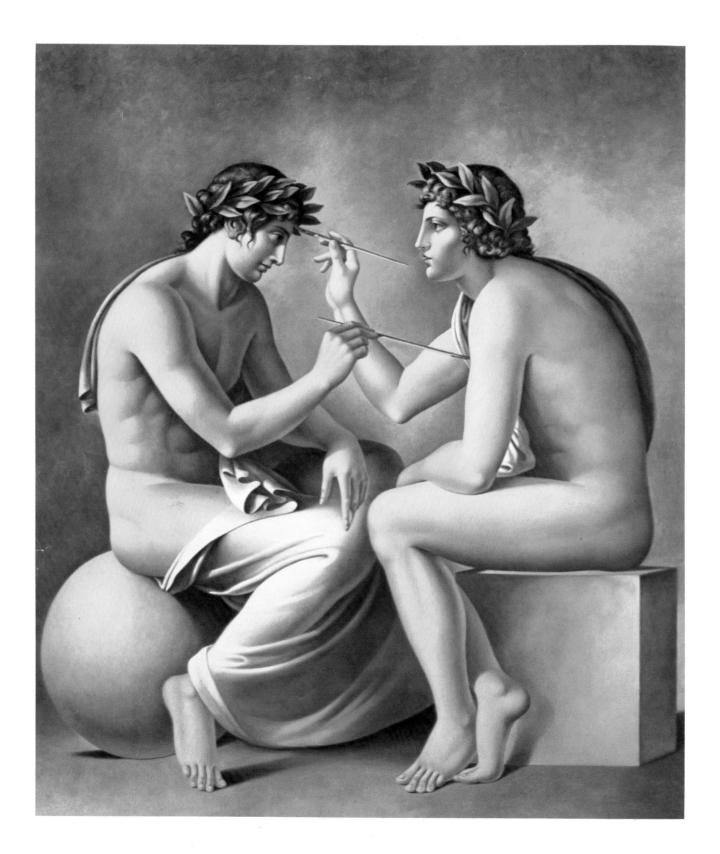

Charles Jencks

What is *Post-Modernism*?

AP ACADEMY EDITIONS

For Maggie
1941-1995

Acknowledgements

What Is Post-Modernism? was first given as a paper at conferences in America and Germany in 1985. This fourth, considerably revised, edition has been carefully reconstructed and put together by Lucy Ryan and Alistair Probert – to them I am grateful. The photographs are credited, as before, in the captions.

COVER: Ron Kitaj, *If Not, Not*, 1975-6, oil on canvas, 152 x 152cm, detail

PAGE 2: Carlo Maria Mariani, *La Mano Ubbidisce all'Intelleto*, 1983, oil on canvas, 199 x 175.5cm

First published in Great Britain in 1986, revised Edition in 1996 by
ACADEMY EDITIONS
An imprint of
ACADEMY GROUP LTD
42 Leinster Gardens, London W2 3AN
Member of the VCH Publishing Group

ISBN: 1 85490 428 0

Distributed to the trade in the USA by
NATIONAL BOOK NETWORK, INC
4720 Boston Way, Lanham, Maryland 20706

Printed and bound in Singapore

CONTENTS

PREFACE TO THE FOURTH EDITION: WHITHER POST-MODERNISM?

Post-Modernism is now a world-wide movement in all the arts and disciplines. Post-modern politics varies from the conviction politics of Margaret Thatcher and Tony Blair to the search for a new liberalism that can combine multiculturalism and universal rights; post-modern food varies from Cambozola (Camembert and Gorgonzola improved by combining) to California Cuisine (French plus Pacific Rim plus supposedly healthy). There are more books appearing today on Post-Modernism than its parent Modernism, which is not to say it is more mature or better, but just here to stay. We are well past the age when we can merely accept or reject this new 'ism'; it is too omnipresent and important for either approach. Rather we have to ask about its emergent possibilities, ask 'What is it?', and then decide selectively to support and criticise aspects of the movement.

This hybrid book started life as a conference paper in 1985 and in subsequent editions became progressively more mongrelised. Now, thanks to a computer which allowed me to reconsider the whole, it is I hope easier to understand if still eclectic. The idea of plurality is essential to Post-Modernism; the necessity of crossing boundaries and mixing genres is also a norm, which I will reaffirm.

The variety of subject matter does mean, however, that the reader will jump between different fields and hear different voices. Philosophy, history, parable, sociology and polemic are intermixed. The first three sections, Part One, define the field and concept of Post-Modernism, the logic of history which makes the use of the term virtually inevitable today. Here I explain why 'post-modern has chosen us' and will not let go.

Part Two focuses on post-modern culture, more particularly architecture, art, philosophy and literature; because of my interests the major focus throughout is architecture. The question I pose, in a parable, is why did modern culture, modern socialism, modern avant-gardism take on the Protestant temper? What caused it to be Puritanical and exclusivist? Why, when the Logical Positivists such as Wittgenstein and Ayer, excommunicated so many philosophers for upholding values or metaphysics, did the Modernists cheer? Why did the Modernists, in their crusade against the Ancients, reject history, sentiment, memory, ornament, context and so much else? To explain the New Protestant Reformation I give something of a psychological answer to these questions and show that it led, ultimately, to the New Counter-Reformation – Post-Modernism. Indeed, I will argue that one of the deep reasons for Post-Modernism is the reassertion of the presence of worldliness, fecundity, variety and embodied spirituality: that is, a cosmic orientation based on contemporary science.

Part Three looks at the shifts in post-modern society, including the decline of the nation-state, the rise of a global civilisation and a series of 'posts' – post-industrial society, Post-Fordism, the post-national economy and Post-Socialism. What is behind all these shifts and slides? Post-modernisation, the change to a global, electronic culture driven by the world economy and communication.

In Part Four, I conclude with an idea that most other observers of the same situation reject: the post-modern period has not seen the end of all metanarratives, but rather their proliferation. We do not live in an era when all beliefs have become non-credible, but rather at the beginning of an emergent global culture with a new metanarrative – the story of the universe. This, I believe, will form the organising principle for historical religions as well as science and other cultural discourses – no small claim. My arguments are taken from the post-modern sciences of complexity as well as recent cosmology. These show the universe to be a single, creative, unfolding event in which life, mind and culture are perfectly natural, probably inevitable. Throughout my narrative I assume that history is not 'just one crazy thing after another' – it has some direction, meaning and even, contrary to Modernist doctrine, purpose. I do not expect everyone to agree with these opinions or others; but they are part of the new world view.

I know an author is allowed one neologism per book and I have broken this rule. The word 'cognitariat' is coined to refer to the new class system emergent in the First World and elsewhere, the 'paraclass' of the new information society which cuts across previous categories; and the word 'socitalism' is coined to refer to the new blend of economic sectors that defines the predominant type – socialised capitalism. Each word is polemical, meant to provoke as it makes one think how inadequate the terms are with which we are stuck – 'bourgeoisie', 'socialism', 'capitalism'. These labels were fashioned about the time of the first steam train, in 1820, and who, today, rides around in one of those? The fact that politicians still triumph on, or sweat blood under, nineteenth-century labels should not coerce the rest of us. So I plead somewhat guilty, but unrepentant.

A final warning before I try to clarify terms. This book was written ten years ago, rewritten in parts and now completely. As such it is a palimpsest, a reminted coin; or, better, a series of ideas that have grown on top of each other like generations of barnacles or coral. This means it is a new type of book that may become more common in an age when the computer allows easy rewriting. Whole sections have been moved, chopped and recombined; perhaps one third of the original remains untouched; attitudes reflect the years 1985, 1987, 1989 and 1995. I like the idea of growing up with one's offspring and, believing that every new genre needs a new name, I would like to christen this a 'transitext', or 'metamorphibook', or 'rescription', or 'evolvotome' – but I doubt such terms would find favour.

A Note About Usage

Since applications of post-modern and modern abound, some initial, short definitions may be useful. The hyphenated phrase post-modern will be used for the cultural movement, emergent morality and social condition; the elided postmodern for the Deconstructivist movement (or where it is used this way by another author); Post-Modernism and Post-Modernists – the movement and its protagonists – are capitalised. These usages derive from post-modernisation, the global, electronic civilisation, its new economy and spacetime implosion.

Modernism (1840 to 1930) is a cultural movement relating directly to modernity – the social condition of living in an urban, fast-changing, progressivist world governed by instrumental reason. This in turn stems from modernisation (continual economic growth dependent on industrialisation and progressive technology).

A fuzzy set of divisions – First, Second, Third and Fourth Worlds – will be used, in spite of their unfortunate hierarchical overtones and lack of accuracy. They classify a mixture of economic, social and cultural factors which can never be very precise. The Fourth World, called 'primitive', native or indigenous one hundred years ago, is disappearing, but still extant. There are six thousand languages today and the predictions are that in thirty years, if modernisation is not slowed, there will be three hundred. The Second World, former communist and socialist nations, has now started to slide in opposite directions, but it still keeps some coherence as a category known otherwise in unwieldy terms as 'economies in transition'. The Third World is 'developing' and is often refered to as such. A further complication is that the First World – the so-called 'Developed' world – is also still modernising and post-modernising.

Synonyms for the First World such as the OECD (Organisation for Economic Co-operation and Development) and Group of Seven are equally problematic. I do not like the terms 'Four Worlds' as labels and I apologise to those who find them offensive, but they are the only well-known terms which have some sense of truth, however fuzzy.

There are approximately two billion people enjoying a relatively modernised standard of living (depending on what economic and social indices are used). These people, the First World plus large parts of the Second and Third, I call the Two-Fifths World – 'us', the people who travel in planes, cars and still read books. The term 'we' is often used with much more limitation to mean a nation, ethnicity, culture, or small group. Through travels to Asian and Muslim societies I – an Anglo-American – have become aware that the slippery terms 'us' and 'we' are both inclusive and inevitably misunderstood. My own national identity, having lived in both the USA and UK for thirty years, is unusual but hardly unique; a blend which is characteristic of an age of migration. Mixed national identity is a consequence of the emergent, global culture, a post-modern phenomenon, which is both international and local.

PART ONE

THE LOGIC OF HISTORY

WHO ARE WE ?

To some critics, the Museum of Modern Art has seemed like an oxymoron, the embodiment of words attributed to Gertrude Stein: 'A museum can be either a museum or it can be modern, but it can't be both.' The Modern must decide whether it will be a voice in contemporary art, or merely a kind of artefact in a post-modern world. (Dinitia Smith, 'New Era Begins at Museum of Modern Art', *International Herald Tribune*, June 17-18, 1995, p8)

In the summer of 1989, forty-eight globe-trotting intellectuals assembled at Boston University to debate a perplexing issue: exactly what period do we inhabit? More simply, who are we? Is there still such a thing as national identity? Are the 'we' that dispute such points still Americans or Frenchmen, Westerners or First Worlders, or have we become the more general *Homo sapiens*? It is a nagging question that will not go away, and more than academic reputations depend on its answer: cultural identity, of course, not to mention such institutional questions as museums called 'Modern', and planning at the United Nations.

Is this still, as it was classified fifty years ago, The Age of Anxiety, or has it finally settled into The Quantum Age of Uncertainty? One global theorist has called it the Quantum Age because discoveries in fundamental particles have changed our view of the universe, and the largest industry in the world is based on quantum electronics. Perhaps, however, it is a period that should be classified by its catastrophes – mass famines, species extinction, Aids, mass-warfare, environmental pollution – or, to be upbeat, its striving – The Era of Space Exploration. Metaphors which classify an age have as much importance as national identity because they orient action, self-understanding and purpose (or lack of it).

Instead of the usual cultural classification, such as the Middle Ages, the Renaissance and so on, our period might be seen in terms of more powerful forces that shape it – politics, social movements, or economics. Then it would be The End of Colonialism, or more recently, the Collapse of Communism, Early Capitalism, or, looking progressively, the epoch when Late-Capitalism arrived (that is, dominance by consumerism and trans-national corporations). Yet, maybe all social and intellectual labels are too anthropomorphic and we really need a transcendent category outside our

[1] Ian Hamilton-Finlay, **Adorno's Hut**, 1986-7 (with Andrew Townsend and Keith Brookwell). The post-modern hybrid that challenges the present with the past and the past with the present. The origins of architecture, in trees and brachiated structures, led to the primitive hut which then led to the classical temple. This logical and evolutionary argument is placed above stylistic integration: the post-modern typically subverts traditions from within through a form of double coding. It accepts conventions in order to criticise and extend the modern, the classical and other traditions. (Antonia Reeve)

human concerns, such as The Age of Gaia or Cosmic Consciousness.

At the Bostonian psychoanalysis of the present, the question marks inevitably triumphed over the labels and, if deep thinkers could agree on anything, ours might be The Age of Queries, or Transition, or Pluralism. We live, to be sure, in a period which is constantly asking itself the big question – 'in which era do we live?' – and one of the ironies is that this question has been posed continuously since the 1820s, since the Moderns became conscious of time as a culturally creative force, of historical identity as something to be understood, analysed, or even, as Karl Marx hoped, changed. Today, as Post-Marxists reformulate the refrain, our identity might be socially reconstructed. 'Who are we?' becomes the existentialist question 'who might we become tomorrow?' This has been a perennial headache since Hamlet interrogated himself on the subject, and certainly since the turn of the century when Paul Gauguin painted his famous questions *D'où venons-nous? Que sommes-nous? Où allons-nous?*

Indeed, given his vision of a primitive paradise – where have we come from and where are we going? – Gauguin's Polynesian women, living close to the earth and other animals, interrogate advanced civilisation and seem to pose an existential choice. But is it possible for 'us' to live like them, more than five billion of us, many of whom are locked into the global marketplace? For two billion (about to be three) modernisation is irreversible; there is no way – short of catastrophe – that we can live like hunter-gatherers, or even like villagers. The three Ms are one-way doors: once you have gone through technical modernisation, social modernity and Cultural Modernism there is no going back. Some theologians have compared this to Original Sin and The Fall, a unidirectional event which entails responsibility, not to say guilt, for what goes on in the Garden. The fundamentalists have it wrong. You cannot unlearn Newton, Darwin and Freud any more than you can repeal the global marketplace, Nietzsche and Ford. Gauguin's questions are basic: 'Where have we come from? What are we? Where are we going?' Social and cognitive developments are sequential, cumulative, inescapable. What choices do we have?

Before we fall deeper into self-scrutiny, become more enveloped by the couch of psychohistory, we might note – as Isaiah Berlin has done – some historical comparisons. Confident nations and individuals already know who they are – or, rather, never think of asking – while insecure ones, caught in transition, have conferences on the Riddle of the Sphinx. There were many books published in late nineteenth-century Russia, such as Chernyshezsky's *What is to be Done?* Now virtually every culture has become late nineteenth-century Russia, particularly late twentieth-century Russia.

This need not necessarily be depressing; Socrates, Christ and Thoreau – to name three self-questioners – made deep introspection into an art of strength. Since two-fifths of the world is now forced onto the couch, might we not learn to cultivate this strength?

POST-MODERN CHOOSES US

The answer to the last rhetorical question must remain personal and situational. If one thing is clear today it is that 'we' is plural, both global and multicultural, likely to be related to the world network of information (if not Internet) while immersed in particular cultures. Precisely because of proliferating globalisation we are made much more conscious of increasing minoritisation. The once dominant American nation, which held some 45 per cent of world trade after 1950, is sinking into tertiary status, not necessarily because it is declining but because the whole world economy is growing proportionately so big. All nations are becoming smaller players within the larger trading blocs that are emerging. 'We' are constantly reminded that the United Nations will soon mean the loose governance of two hundred nations, that the nation-state is becoming ever weaker and that five thousand would-be nation-states, such as Bosnia, are waiting in the wings to be granted their identity, status and legal rights. 'We' indeed; how inescapable are the quote-marks which emphasise the ever-increasing pluralism and minoritisation and what must come with them – the questioning of self?

Yet, if 'we' are confused and undergoing a millennial-life-crisis and cannot find a fitting label to summarise the period, it does not mean that the label cannot find us. But, could a word pick us, the most free-thinking of species? Language, as many have observed this century, is a social contract which no one writes. Like the economy or fashion, words emerge and are socially accepted through use and reuse. In this conventional sense 'post-modern' has already chosen us, and did so sometime in the mid-eighties, or at least chose a good deal of the conference-attending, writing, reading, chattering, film-going, Sunday Supplement thinking public. Is there anyone outside these categories – at least in the two-fifths world (to insist on our social-economic status)? Yes, of course. A lot of people do not read and have been spared the media-drenching by *Postmodernismo* (1934), Post-Modern (1947), POSTmodernISM (1971), *Postmodernismus* (1977), postmodernism (current in USA 1980), Po-Mo (current in the USA 1985) and all the cognate terms. They are here to stay.[1]

Let us ironise our fallen state into mediafication before we analyse what it may mean. Few people welcome the term. It is today unfashionable,

[2] Alessandro Mendini, **Groningen Museum**, Groningen, Holland, 1990-4 – post-modern or PO-MO? The break up of the museum into a village of pavilions, designed by different architects, reflects the heterogeneity of a city today (as well as this museum's collection of opposed cultural periods). The juxtaposition of styles, spaces and materials on an island is inventive and fresh – but some of the architecture? Close to graphics and the sweet stink of Warholian PO-MO. (C Jencks)

1 The most scholarly studies of the term include Margaret Rose, *The Post-Modern and The Post-Industrial, A Critical Analysis*, Cambridge University Press, 1991 and Wolfgang Welsch, *Unsere postmoderne Moderne*, VCH (Weinheim), 1988 and Hans Bertens, *The Idea of the Postmodern*, Routledge (London), 1995.

SEVENTY POSTS

(I) PREHISTORY – 1870-1950 POST-MODERN AS MODERN PERIOD IN DECLINE (OR RARELY) ULTRA-MODERN

Post-Modern, 1870-1914, John Watkins Chapman, Rudolf Pannwitz
Post-Industrialism, 1914-22, Arthur J Penty
postmodernismo, 1934, Federico de Onis
post-Modernism, 1945, Bernard Smith
post-modern house, 1945, Joseph Hudnut
Post-Modern Age, 1939/1946, Arnold Toynbee
Postmodern poets, 1946, Randall Jarrell
Post-Historic Man, 1950, Roderick Seidenberg
post-Modern sciences, 1954, Arnold Toynbee
postmodernism, 1954, Charles Olson
Postmodern Fiction as Decline, 1959, Irving Howe, 1960 Harry Levin
post-capitalism, 1959, Ralf Dahrendorf

(II) 1950-80 PM DEFINED POSITIVELY AS COUNTER CULTURE, DOUBLE-CODING, 'POSTS', PLURALISM AND DECREATION

postbourgeois, 1963, George Lichtheim
postmodernist worldly writers, 1963, William van O'Connor
post-civilisation, 1964, Kenneth Boulding
post-scarcity economy, 1966
Post-Modern religion, 1968, John Cobb
Post-humanist anti-elitism, 1965, Leslie Fiedler
post-modern period, 1968, Amitai Etzioni
Poststructuralism, 1969, Jacques Derrida
post-collectivist politics, 1969, Sam Beer
post-liberal era, 1969, Sir Geoffrey Vickers
Post-Christian, 1970, Sydney E Ahlstrom
post-ideology, 1970, Lewis Feuer
post-traditional societies, 1970, SN Eisenstadt
post-economic man, 1970, Herman Kahn
post-tribal societies, 1971, Eric Hobsbawm
POSTmodernISM/mystical silence, 1971/1975, Ihab Hassan
Postmodern American poetry, 1971, David Antin
Postmodern literature, 1972, William Spanos
Post-Marxism, 1973, Daniel Bell
Postmodern American poetics, 1973, Charles Altieri
Post-Industrial Society, 1973, Daniel Bell

2 To show the fast and furious pace of the term, I will mention three of the seventeen which appeared recently. My own *The Post-Modern Reader*, Academy/St Martins Press (London/New York), 1992, has thirty articles varying from post-modern film to science and religion; Thomas Docherty's *PoStmOdErNnism, A Reader*, Harvester Wheatsheaf (Hemel Hempstead), 1993, has thirty-four articles varying from post-modern politics to avant-gardism; Joseph Natoli and Linda Hutcheon, *A Postmodern Reader*, Suny Press (Albany), 1993, has twenty-five articles varying from 'postmodern blackness' to 'The Postmodern *weltanschauung*'. Three 'readers' with some overlap of authors appeared within twelve months of each other – it never happened with Modernism, even in its heyday. Yet the press tend to magnify the less savoury aspects of Postmodernism; the deconstructive nihilism of some philosophers or that of consumer society, eg *TLS*, 16 October and 18 December, 1992 and *The Independent* on Sunday, 16 November, 1992, p21.

inelegant and yet, for all that, inescapable. It has stuck to us socially – a badge to be worn with pride, or a shameful brand. There are indeed a few of us who will use the term positively to signify an emergent morality and cultural agenda. This brief treatise will show how elements of such a new world view have grown from architecture, philosophy and the arts.

Positive movement, negative condition or just plain description, there are more conferences, books, scholarly papers and lead articles on the phrase every year. Like it or not it has become the focus for debate about the present, for discussion of where we are and how we got here, for the main choices and issues facing us. As soon as the debate starts – where are we now? – the concepts of the modern and then post-modern follow like a well-conditioned reflex. In this sense, both concepts have achieved a kind of intellectual lock-in.

The notion of lock-in is well developed in biology, product design and technology. For instance, the keyboard I am writing on – QWERTY (the first six letters of the 1890s' typewriter) – achieved lock-in one hundred years ago, in spite of being sub-optimal from several functional standpoints. Now computers which have no movable gears (the prime reason for QWERTY) and other machines follow this convention. Any species or product always shows this mixture of universal function and contingent compromise, and both get locked-in by evolutionary development. We will see the logical reasons why 'post-modern' – suboptimal though it may be in certain respects – achieved lock-in sometime in the 1980s.

A mere list of 'pm titles' would fill a thousand pages; a bibliography would become a small encyclopaedia. In spite of the dislike of the phrase it has become the label for seventeen anthologies I have, and a search on Internet would probably produce another fifty.[2] The term is now almost as ubiquitous, disliked and misunderstood as its parent, the modern. By 1992, the British *Independent* recommended Post-modernism because it meant anything you care to think about the present.

If this social usage is irreversible, its semantic logic is equally compelling. Since 'modern' comes from the Latin *modo* meaning 'just now', 'post-modern' obviously means 'after' just now – or sometimes beyond, contra, above, ultra, meta, outside-of the present. This attack on the present tense is motivated by the idea of living across time, in an historical and cultural continuum that stretches into the future. It is always a denial of the flatness of what is called 'presentism', and an insistence that memory and evolution are built very importantly into the universe in a way that cultural Modernism often denies. This is the 'post' relating to 'posterity'; the desire to live across cultural zones and time. It is also a rebuttal of nostalgia because, while acknowledging the past, it does so in a way which is non-revivalist and ironic. We are as much 'post' the past (traditional culture) as the modern.

The psycho-logic of being 'post' is that of transcendence, so there are spiritual and political overtones to the term. Going beyond the modern means, in spatial terms, to get above or outside the present. One should not underrate this desire, the most potent of the inherent meanings.

The phrase thus carries the weight of all the 'posties' that have been around since the 1880s and Post-Impressionism: post-industrial, post-historic, Post-Capitalist, Post-Christian, etc (see diagram **Seventy Posts**). Common to all these usages is the notion of posteriority, the transition from a known classifier to an unknown but suggestive future. Post-Christianity implies Christianity evolving on a global scale into some new hybrid philosophy – something that keeps the valuable teachings of Christ, but cuts away incredible beliefs and orients to a cosmic and evolutionary future.[3]

Post-modern has chosen us because it is so precise and ambiguous at the same time; accurate about the port we have left and richly suggestive of the destiny for which we are heading. The direction comes from the past cultural weighting and the pull of the future. It has, as its essential definition, what I have called a double coding. For me the post-modern is the continuation of modernity and its transcendence. In this sense it is critical.[4]

It is very important to stress this subtle relationship to Modernism because so many misunderstand it. Post-Modernism is not Anti-Modernism; it is neither traditionalism nor the reactionary rejection of its parent. It does not, as the philosophers Jurgen Habermas and Jean-François Lyotard contend, reject the Enlightenment project; that is, the social emancipation of humanity, increasing freedom and universal rights. Rather, it rejects the totalising arguments with which universal rights are often imposed by an elite on a subservient minority (along with so much else). Modern liberalism fought for the 'universal' rights which the First World now partly enjoys; post-modern liberalism argues that the agenda of multiculturalism, and the rights of minorities should be asserted where they do not diminish the rights of other minorities. In this sense it is the direct heir of its parent and could not have occurred previously. It is quite true that the logic of modern and post-modern liberalism are different, and sometimes in conflict, but that does not make either of them invalid. They are both necessary to the concept of justice in society.

Furthermore, there is a genetic connection between the two camps. The initial Post-Modernists in literature, architecture and philosophy were first trained with the tenets and methods of Modernism, and then went beyond

Post-Modern Architecture, 1975, Charles Jencks
post-modern dance, 1975, Michael Kirby
Post-Modern science,1976, Frederick Ferre/Stephen Toulmin
 postmodernismus, 1977, Michael Kohler/Jurgen Peper
post-materialism, 1977
Deconstructive postmodernism, 1979
La Condition Postmodern, 1979, Jean-François Lyotard
Postmodern fiction as replenishment, 1980, John Barth

(III) 1980+ PM CONDITION ATTACKED, PM CULTURE ANTHOLOGISED, PM GLOBAL MORALITY DEFINED

postminimalism, 1979
post-performance art, 1980s
Post-Modernity Destroys Meaning, 1981, Jean Baudrillard
postmodern sublime, 1982, Jean-François Lyotard
Post-National Economies, 1983
Postmodern pluralism, 1983, Matei Calinescu
Postmodern irony & enjoyment, 1983, Umberto Eco
Postmodernism, The Cultural Logic of Late-Capitalism
    1984, Frederic Jameson
Post-Fordism, 1984
Post-Feminism, 1984
Postmodern *weltanschauung*, 1984, Hans Bertens
Postmodern culture, 1984, Hal Foster
Po-Mo, 1985, pejorative phrase in use
Post-Logical Positivism, 1985, Mary Hesse
Post-Modern Aura, 1985, Charles Newman
Constructive Postmodernism, 1986, David Ray Griffin
postmodern excremental culture, 1986, Kroker/Crook
postmodern politics, 1986, J Arac
Post-Darwinism, 1987
Postmodern society, 1987, Scott Lash, Anthony Giddens
Postmodern poetics, 1988, Linda Hutcheon
Postmodern geography, 1988, Edward Soja
The Condition of Postmodernity, 1989, David Harvey
Post-Cold War, 1989
Post-history, 1990, Francis Fukuyama
Ecological postmodernism, 1989, Charles Birch/Charlene
    Spretnak
Postmodern global ethic, 1991, Hans Kung
Post-Modern agenda, 1992, Charles Jencks
Postmodern Ethics & Morality, 1992-3, Zygmunt Bauman

[3] **Three Phases of Post-Modern**. *The first use of the phrase was unsystematic and often referred to a new period when the modern lost its direction. The second period defined the concept positively in terms of pluralism, decentering, and counter-cultures, while the third phase analysed the negative postmodern condition and the various positive post-modern movements. In general, the social condition is lower case and streamlined, the movements are upper case and hyphenated. Texts are italicised that I find either the most significant or influential.*

3 'Post-Christianity' has the ambivalence of all the posts as it implies that Christianity can be renewed in radical ways which still keep important foundations.

4 I first used this definition of double coding in 1978 articles and books to distinguish Post-Modernism from the new tradition with which it was being confused – Late-Modernism. For a discussion *see* Margaret Rose, *The Post-Modern and The Post-Industrial, A Critical Analysis*, Cambridge University Press, 1991.

[4] Bernard Tschumi, **Parc de la Villette**, 1984. One of the first 'red points' in Tschumi's abstract grid is this 'folie' in the Late-Constructivist Style. The revival of twenties Modernism, in an extreme form, is often mistaken for Post-Modernism. (C Jencks)

this training by going back to the past, or sideways to a local culture, or anywhere outside the present tense of space and time. They did this to build another tradition, something better. Yet, by definition, they always kept their other half; hence the hybrid, and hyphen, in post-modern.

There is, however, another postmodernism equally logical, accepted and conventionally written without the hyphen. This, the streamlined edition, usually means a society that has either fragmented or become a consumerist hyper-reality, or both. Philosophically and psychologically it expresses a condition of doubt. Often this streamlined version means a deconstructionist movement which purports to resist Disneyworld culture: Jacques Derrida, Michel Foucault, Jean Baudrillard, Frederic Jameson – and their sometime-philosopher-king, Jean-François Lyotard. Every American academic knows these Five Wise Decons because they have become, not surprisingly, Kings in the Land of Tenured Scepticism. Their reign will certainly survive my irony; they fit as snugly into the Age of Agnosticism as devout clerics in the Age of Faith.

There is one more psychological impetus to the term. If modern means 'up to date' and is used unselfconsciously this way by everybody, then it has a privileged grasp on the notion of progress. In this sense modern computers are the latest generation, the most highly developed, the most powerful, subtle and adept. They are immediately privileged over all previous generations in so far as we assume a progressive view of technology and evolution (which is to say very far). Thus post-modern naturally carries the psychological suggestion of being even more up to date, Modernism + 1 – Supermodernism – and this implicit trump card (with its added suggestion of overturning) is why Modernists continue to get so angry with the term. It seems to render them old fashioned according to the same logic with which they had consigned tradition, the past, and local cultures to the scrap heap of superstitions. It uses very modernist tactics against the Modernists, declaring a culture obsolescent. One does not have to subscribe to these views and tactics to see why they are so effective in a political sense. For one thing they allowed the modern to be declared 'dead' and seen as an historical period, rather than the most up-to-date, and that allowed many creative movements to occur, not just post-modern ones.[5]

5 The architectural historian John Summerson wrote of Post-Modernism that its most creative and liberating idea was the 'death' of Modernism. The death certificate certainly opened a lot of doors onto the future, not just pm ones, since it denied that Modernism had the only claim to the present, its totalising pretence.

CAPSULE HISTORY

As a rough guide to the two basic kinds of Post-Modernism (often with and without hyphen), it is useful to keep a brief history in mind. According to Wolfgang Welsch the first inconsequential use of the term was as early as the 1870s, by the British artist John Watkins Chapman, but it was really the social concept 'post-industrial' which was first theorised by Arthur J Penty and others, from 1914-22.[6] And here we find a recurrent confusion. Because of the same prefix, there is a tendency to lump all 'posts' together as if there were one giant, homogeneous movement – a *Zeitgeist*, or totalistic period – whereas in fact, according to Post-Modernism itself, pluralism reigns. Indeed, traditional, modern and late and post-modern sensibilities may overlap in the same culture. There is not one dominant world view or *epistemé* in the globe today; all are running concurrently.

The first, tentative, written use of Post-Modernism was apparently that of the Spanish writer Federico de Onis. In his *Antología de la poesia española e hispanoamericana*, 1934, he used it to describe a reaction from within Modernism, not a critical overcoming of the paradigm. Subsequently, Arnold Toynbee, in his *A Study of History*, 1947, used the term as an encompassing category to describe a new historical cycle starting in 1875. This formulated the end of Western dominance, the decline of individualism, capitalism and Christianity, and the rise to power of non-Western cultures. In addition, it referred in a positive way to a pluralism and world culture, meanings which are still essential to its definition today. But Toynbee was, on the whole, sceptical of the decline implicit in the prefix 'Post' and it is interesting that this scepticism was shared by the literary critics Irving Howe and Harold Levine, who first used the term polemically. Their essentially negative description has stayed with the movement.

Since then, the phrase has continued to work in a double way – as both a scourge and a challenge, an insult and a slogan to be carried into battle.[7] Consider the irony; Howe and Levine's usage, in 1959 and 1960, was – as EH Gombrich has shown of the first use of the terms Gothic, Mannerism, Baroque, Rococo and Romanesque – malevolent enough to sting, but potent enough to catch on and become positive.[8] Labels, like the movements they describe, often have this paradoxical power – to issue fruitfully from the mouths of detractors. As we will see with the modern inquisition of post-modern architects, the paranoia of the persecutors can be unintentionally useful for the persecuted.

Virtually the first positive use of the prefix 'post' was by the writer Leslie Fiedler in 1965, when he repeated it like an incantation and tied it to current radical trends which made up the counter-culture: 'post-humanist, post-male,

6 For this source *see* Margaret Rose, *The Post-Modern and The Post-Industrial, A Critical Analysis*, Cambridge University Press, 1991.

7 *See* Irving Howe, 'Mass Society and Postmodern Fiction' (1963) in *The Decline of the New*, Harcourt Brace and World (New York), 1970. *The Decline of the New*, as the title suggests, also treats the subject of Modernist decline into Postmodernism. *See also* Gerald Graff, 'The Myth of the Postmodern Breakthrough' reprinted in *Literature Against Itself*, The University of Chicago Press, (Chicago and London), 1979. Graff's critique of the post-modern seems to be more aptly directed at late-modern literature, as I mentioned to him when we met at a conference in Evanston, 1985 (which gave birth to this book). But he is using the term as defined by Howe, Levin, Charles Olsen, Hassan and others. For Harold Levin *see* 'What was Modernism?', *Refractions: Essays in Comparative Literature*, Oxford University Press (New York), 1966.

8 For this idea and a discussion of several terms *see* EH Gombrich, 'The Origins of Stylistic Terminology', *Norm and Form*, Phaidon (London), 1966, pp83-6, and 'Mannerism: The Historiographic Background', also printed in *Norm and Form*, pp99-106.

[5] Peter Blake, **The Meeting** or **Have a Nice Day Mr Hockney**, 1981-3, oil on canvas, 99 x 124.5cm. An ironic meeting of 1960s 'Pop' painters at the post-modern academy in the 1980s. This new version of Courbet's The Meeting or Bonjour Monsieur Courbet is both a contemporary comment on Classicism and a classical composition in itself. The meeting is between three representational artists – Howard Hodgkin, Peter Blake and David Hockney – the last with a brush rather than a staff in his hand. The squatting girl's pose is taken partly from a skating magazine and partly from classical sculpture. The heroic meeting in 'Venice', California, commemorates an historical act, if not a grand public one, as the nineteenth-century Classicist would no doubt have preferred. Monumentality and banality, a timeless present and the transient afternoon are set in serene contrast. (Courtesy of the Tate Gallery, London)

post-white, post-heroic . . . post-Jewish'.[9] These anarchic and creative departures from orthodoxy; these attacks on modernist elitism, academicism and puritanical repression, represent the first stirrings of post-modern culture, although Fiedler and others in the 1960s were never to put this argument as such and conceptualise the tradition.[10] Like the Pop artists and architects, Post-Modernists wanted to reach a large and variegated audience without slipping into populism. A positive defence of the growing tradition had to wait until the 1970s and the writings of Ihab Hassan, by which time the radical movements which Fiedler celebrated were, ironically, out of fashion, reactionary, or dead.

By the mid-seventies, Ihab Hassan had become the self-proclaimed spokesman for the postmodern and he tied this label to the ideas of experimentalism in the arts and ultra-technology in architecture. His list of exemplars includes William Burroughs and Buckminster Fuller, and such key terms as 'Anarchy, Exhaustion/Silence . . . Decreation/Deconstruction/ Antithesis . . . Inter-text . . . ' These are the trends which I, with others, would later characterise as late-modern, because they took modernist impulses to an extreme. In literature and then in philosophy, because of the writings of Jean-François Lyotard in 1979 and a tendency to elide Deconstruction with the post-modern, the term has often kept associations with what Hassan calls 'discontinuity, indeterminacy, immanence'.[11] Mark C Taylor's curiously titled *ERRING, A Postmodern A/Theology* is characteristic of this genre, which springs from Derrida and Deconstruction.[12]

My own *The Language of Post-Modern Architecture*, 1977, was the first book to thematise a post-modern movement and use the phrase in the title. This, coupled with the fact that the architectural movement was directed and visibly coherent, led many people to say that I invented the term and concept, a claim that is true only in the sense that I theorised, popularised and gave it a book title. What I did was to summarise the various responses to the architectural failures of modernity and tie them polemically to a wide agenda of double-coding. The success (and failure) of this polemical act will be apparent shortly, but it also had the effect of amplifying nascent movements in philosophy and the arts which were seen as related. Because of this, and the writings of Hassan and then Lyotard, the movement quickly became a self-fulfilling prophecy and moved right off – exploding in the 1980s to become a series of deconstructive and post-structuralist schools or, by contrast, movements that were self-styled 'contextual', 'constructive', 'ecological', 'grounded' and 'restructive' post-modernism.[13]

It is clear from this capsule history that two basic movements exist, as well as 'the post-modern condition': 'reactionary postmodernism' and 'consumer

9 *See* Leslie Fiedler, 'The New Mutants' (1965) in *The Collected Essays of Leslie Fiedler, Vol 11*, Stein and Day (New York), 1970, and *A Fiedler Reader*, Stein and Day (New York), 1977, pp189-210.

10 *See* Andreas Huyssen, 'Mapping the Postmodern', *New German Critique, No 33*, Fall 1984, devoted to Modernity and Postmodernity, University of Wisconsin (Milwaukee), 1984.

11 *See* Ihab Hassan, 'The Question of Postmodernism', *Romanticism, Modernism, Postmodernism*, Harry R Garvin (ed), Bucknell University Press (Lewisberg, Toronto and London), 1980, pp117-26.

12 *See* Mark C Taylor, *ERRING, A Postmodern A/Theology*, The University of Chicago Press (Chicago and London), 1984.

13 David Ray Griffin has edited the SUNY series on 'Constructive Postmodern Thought', so termed to distinguish it from deconstructive, or eliminative postmodernism. Due to the numerous modern movements, our group, the Portrack Seminars, has coined several alternatives. Charlene Spretnak and Charles Birch favour 'ecological postmodernism'; others favour the hybrid 'restructive postmodernism' combining the constructive and restructing; I favour using a hyphen and dropping the prefix, but some marker is needed to distinguish the two main types.

[6] **Modernisation Anywhere**. *The erosion of the city and countryside, the force of economic growth and the style of instrumental reason – these are the universals of modernity. (C Jencks)*

postmodernism'; for example, the information age, the Pope and Madonna (all of whom have been written about in these very terms). If one wants an impartial guide through this complex territory, Margaret Rose's *The Post-Modern and the Post-Industrial: A Critical Analysis*, 1991, serves quite well.

I reiterate that one of the great strengths of the word and the concept, and why it will probably be potent for another hundred years, is that it is carefully suggestive of our having gone beyond the inadequate world-view of Modernism without specifying exactly where we are going. That is why most people will spontaneously use the term, as if for the first time, to overcome the era and world view they wish to transcend. They are convinced the Modern is not the Eternal.

Along with the geologist Thomas Berry, we might take an even longer view than one hundred years and say it is not just the modern age which is ending, but the incomprehensibly vast time span of the Cenozoic.[14] This geological period has lasted sixty-five million years – since the dinosaurs became extinct, along with 75 per cent of the other contemporaneous species. Looking at history this way really is the larger view; one that focuses on much longer time-spans, or 'waves', than historians, economists, especially Marxists, consider relevant. Their economic wavelets of four hundred years ride on huge ecological tidal waves. We are now again at the beginning of another period of turbulence, another mass extinction, the sixth in the last six hundred million years. And what is one cause? A modernity that is much too successful, a modernisation that China, India, Latin America and Africa desperately want to achieve. Whatever happens, they are going to try very hard to approach our consumption levels, and this rampant modernisation will continue to create in response, and for as far as we can see, various post-modern movements. To take this sixty-five million year view is dwarfing. It provides a negative push towards the bigger cosmic picture, a complement to the positive pull brought about, quite independently, by the emergent sciences of complexity. These constitute what I believe is the heart of Post-Modernism. Before looking at this big canvas we might first examine the relatively small world of global architecture, where the post-modern movement coalesced. The battle between Modernism and Post-Modernism first erupted in this profession because it is most engaged, by necessity, with the contradictions of modernisation. We can approach this through a mixture of modes typical of Post-Modernism – history, criticism, philosophy – and a little parable.

14 *See* Brian Swimme and Thomas Berry, *The Universe Story, From the Primordial Flaring Forth to the Ecozoic Era*, Harper (San Francisco), 1992; *see also* Thomas Berry's *The Dream of the Earth*, Sierra Club Books (San Francisco), 1988.

PART TWO

POST-MODERN CULTURE

THE PROTESTANT CRUSADE

Modernism is one of the strongest religions – indeed, in the nineteenth century it was the most potent of Post-Christian faiths. With the rise of secularism, Darwinism and atheism and the attacks on Christianity of Feuerbach, Marx and Nietzsche, most intellectuals became sceptics. Following them, much of the Western public became schizophrenic. Many people wanted to believe in a transcendent entity but, given the obvious triumph of materialism on the social scene and its different kinds of theoretical explanations by Adam Smith, Darwin and Marx, they were unable to have wholehearted faith in a Creator. Nationalism, socialism and Marxism quickly filled the vacuum as pseudo-religions; that is, as secular faiths without a full theology or claims to be one. Nevertheless, these ideologies worked beautifully as religions; unquestioned foci for everyday behaviour. Some argue that today the economy is the pseudo-religion. The typical Englishman and American, as can be seen by their behaviour, assumes that economic calculations come first, or last, or always.[15] The bottom line becomes the new Holy Ghost (or vice versa).

Yet this centre of value, or organising principle of society, cannot be named because it is too obviously preposterous: 'I believe in one God Almighty, maker of Heaven and GNP'. This lacks something. It does not sound right. Here, Modernism is much more successful; it is general, and believable as an evolutionary force; it fares better without a Nicene Creed; it works wonders because it is vague – like a Rorschach blob. Modernists project onto the 'ism' all sorts of sacred qualities, wish-fulfilments that Christianity previously absorbed. *Pace* Marx and Aron, it is Modernism that is the 'opiate of the intellectuals'.

By the 1920s the Modern Movement crystallised out of Modernism into a calling, a named prophetic faith in the future. Nietzsche had been here with his Superman, his 'Future Man', overcoming the present; Marxists had formulated their eschatology – the future rule of the proletariat; Futurists since the French Revolution had written books on the year 2,000, forecasting a social transformation, the secular version of the New Jerusalem and the Second Coming; Lenin, under a pseudonym, plotted his communist revolution and Le Corbusier, under his *nom de guerre*, cooked up the architectural one. In 1921 he started what he called a 'crusade' for the new architecture, guided by his magazine, *L'Esprit Nouveau*, basically an instalment-plan bible where the new spirit appeared regularly in every field,

[7] Le Corbusier, **Villa Savoye**, Poissy, France, 1929-33. Pure white forms, according to Le Corbusier's description elevated above an unhealthy ground, are seen in a salubrious and ravishing sunlight. (C Jencks)

15 John Cobb, the Process Theologian who also coined the concept 'Post-Modern religion', 1968, argues that today the economy works as an unconscious religion; from an unpublished presentation to Portrack Seminar, Scotland, 1994.

[8] Mies van der Rohe, **Federal Center**, Chicago, 1964-5. 'Industrialization will solve the social, economic, technical and artistic problems of our time' – Or create them? Mies' late black style of regimented industrialisation, forged in 1933 for the Nazi Reichsbank, triumphed in corporate America during the 1960s. 'The one-percent for art', dropped in the public plaza to humanise an otherwise windswept blackness became a preferred method of sweetening the corporate pill. Seen through modernist eyes this is heroic honesty, absolute integrity, ultimate rigour. But think: this plaza and its red Calder sit in the centre of government. Civic functions, courtrooms, one's relation to the state and fellow citizens – all incarcerated in this modernist anonymity run amok. (C Jencks)

16 Le Corbusier, *Towards a New Architecture*, translated from the French by Frederick Etchells, The Architectural Press (London), 1959, first translation 1927, p12.

17 Ludwig Mies van der Rohe, 'Industrialized Building', 1924, reprinted in *Programmes and Manifestos on 20th Century Architecture*, Lund Humphries (London), 1970, p81.

18 Colin Rowe, *The Architecture of Good Intentions*, Academy Editions (London), 1994, has now been published, nine years after these words were first written.

from body health to mechanised design to abstract painting. Where was this new faith centred? 'A great epoch has begun', Le Corbusier proclaimed:

> There exists in this world a new spirit; it is to be met with particularly in industrial production . . . We must create the mass-production spirit. The spirit of constructing mass-production houses. The spirit of living in mass-production houses. The spirit of conceiving mass-production houses.[16]

Was this spirit Protestant? The idea that living in pure, white washing machines can improve life? So convinced was this prophet of the beneficent effects of a well-designed environment that he ended his bible – *Towards a New Architecture* – with the exhortation: 'Architecture or Revolution . . . It is a question of building which is at the root of the social unrest of today: Architecture or Revolution. Revolution can be avoided.'

Lenin would have laughed. But Walter Gropius, another militant saint of the Design Reformation, founded the Bauhaus as a 'cathedral of the future', and in 1923 declared the standard creed: 'art and technology: a new unity'. Mies van der Rohe made any number of pleas to the Spirit of the Age, the *Zeitgeist* of industrialisation and gave, in 1924, the most extreme formulation of the new faith: 'If we succeed in carrying out this industrialization [of the building process] then the social, economic, technical, and also artistic problems will be readily solved'.[17] Modernisation indeed! But what about sex and power – were they too not on the Protestant agenda?

In spite of this oversight, the three leading modern architects not only practised a Calvinist style, but also believed that if their faith were to govern industrialisation then it could change the world for the better, physically and spiritually. After 1927, and their joint exhibition at Stuttgart, the religion of Modernism spread around the globe to be disseminated by the apostles, and knighted saints, Sir Nikolaus Pevsner, Sir James Richards, Sir Leslie Martin. The orthodox bible of the movement was *Space, Time and Architecture* by Siegfried Giedion.

Modern seminaries were formed at the major universities such as Cambridge and Harvard and from there the Purist doctrines of John Calvin Corbusier, Martin Luther Gropius and John Knox van der Rohe were dispersed. Their white cathedrals, the black and white boxes of the International Style, were soon built in every land, and for a while (until 1960) the people and professors kept the faith. Ornament, polychromy, metaphor, humour, symbolism, place, cultural identity, urban context and convention were put on the Index and all forms of decoration and historical reference were declared taboo. We are all well acquainted with the results – 'the architecture of good intentions' – as Colin Rowe termed them,[18] and there are a lot of pleasant white housing estates and machine-aesthetic hospitals to prove that the intentions were not altogether misguided.

The reigning tenet of architectural Modernism could be called pragmatic amelioration; that is, the belief that by 'doing more with less', as Buckminster Fuller said, social problems would slowly disappear. Technical progress in limited spheres, such as air travel, seems to bear out this ideology, still a dominant one of Late-Modernists (again with their knighted exemplars, Sir Denys Lasdun, Sir Norman Foster, Sir Richard Rogers, Sir . . .). Before continuing this little parable, however inadequate, we might formulate a concise definition. *Modern architecture is the overpowering faith in industrial progressivism and its translation into the pure, white International Style (or at least the Machine Aesthetic) with the goal of transforming society both in its sensibility and social make-up.*

Yet there is something terribly wrong, or at least most curious, here; an anomaly with this Modernism that is both overwhelming and missed by commentators. It is the direct opposite of the more widespread Modernism in the other arts and philosophy, for these are not optimistic and progressivist at all. Think of Nietzsche, Goedel, Heisenberg, Heidegger and Sartre – they were closer to 'might makes right' or nihilism or uncertainty than to the positivism of Fuller. Or think of Yeats, Joyce, Pound, TS Eliot, or De Chirico, Picasso, Duchamp and Grosz. They were hardly liberal, not very socialist and certainly not optimistic. Whereas Modernism in architecture has furthered the ideology of industrialisation and progress, Modernism in most other fields has either fought these trends or lamented them.

However, the various Modernisms agree in two key areas, and that is over the value of abstraction and the overriding importance of aesthetics. Why abstraction? Why do Calvinists resist the image, why do puritans reject the senses, why do iconoclasts prefer white architecture, why do Cistercians like the *tabula rasa*, why do engineers like rationality, why do technicians eschew history? Elimination, purification and abstraction share basic psychological overtones.

As defined by its high American priest, Clement Greenberg, Modernism always has this irreducible goal: to focus on the essence of each art language. By doing this, he argues, standards are kept high in an age of secularisation, where there are few shared values and little left of a common symbolic system. All one can do in this agnostic age of consumer pluralism is sharpen the tools of one's trade, or 'purify the language of the tribe', as Mallarmé and TS Eliot defined the poet's role. It is either one thing or the other or, as Greenberg put it in the key modernist credo of 1939, 'the alternative is

[9] Alvar Aalto, **Tuberculosis Sanatorium**, *Paimio, Finland, 1933. The most appropriate and successful use of the International Style was on hospitals and, occasionally, in Germany, Finland and Switzerland, on workers' housing. With its open-air communal block set amid the pine trees giving the patients salubrious views of nature, and its careful detailing and construction, the Paimio Sanatorium has turned institutional imagery into a heroic reality. (D Porphyrios)*

between Avant-Garde and Kitsch.'

Where did this notion come from? How did the theological role of the avant-garde arise? After the French Revolution, in the early nineteenth century, the idea of a totalistic intellectual elite was born, an avant-garde that would be an integration of as many adjectives as one could credibly string together; it would be artistic, socialistic, positivistic, political, theological and so forth. This intelligentsia, like the famous image of *Liberty at the Barricades*, would beckon followers over the hurdles. As Henri de Saint-Simon, soldier and founder of the concept, said:

> It is we, artists, who will serve you as the avant-garde: the power of the artist is in fact most immediate and most rapid: when we wish to spread new ideas among men, we inscribe them on marble or canvas . . . what is lacking to the arts [today] is that which is essential to their energy and to their success, namely, a common drive and a general idea.[19]

The 'common drive and general idea' was socialism tied to a revolutionary aesthetic. Thus in 1825, the myth of a romantic advance guard, setting out before the rest of society to conquer new territory, new states of consciousness and social order, was formulated. In the history of Modernism since then, there might be few artists who were really politically active, such as Gustave Courbet, and even fewer that were agitating politically, as did Fillipo Marinetti. The ideal, however, lived on; the combination 'new politics + new art' justified the Constructivist designers, legitimising virtually every Modern 'ism' until the 1960s. Furthermore, to be truly *avant* the *arrière*, the avant-garde had to recognise its mission, its crusade. As again Saint-Simon said, echoing the prophetic nature of his name:

> What a most beautiful destiny for the arts, that of exercising over society a positive power, a truly priestly function, and of marching forcefully in the van of all intellectual faculties, in the epoch of their greatest development! This is the duty of artists, this their mission . . .[20]

Thus the avant-garde as the new priesthood, thus progressivist/new art as the harbinger. Here was a role which was elevating and understandable – a mission for a social group that was fast becoming a patronless class. Artists, like architects, were often underemployed and at the mercy of a heartless economic system. Where before they had a defined social relationship to a patron – the State, Church or an individual – now they related to a marketplace that was competitive and agnostic.

In this sense, Modernism is the first ideological response to social crisis and the breakdown of a shared religion. Faced with a Post-Christian society, the creative elite formulated a new role for themselves; inevitably a religious one.

19 Henri de Saint-Simon, *Opinions littéraires, philosophiques et industrielles*, Paris, 1825, quoted in Donald Drew Egbert, *Social Radicalism in the Arts: Western Europe*, Alfred A Knopf (New York), 1970, p121.

20 Ibid, pp121-2.

But, to ask the leading question, how did this crusade become Protestant? By protesting against the dreaded academic bourgeoisie, the arrière-garde; by protesting against ostentatious 'ruling class taste'; by attacking the notion of different styles (Le Corbusier called them 'a lie', Frank Lloyd Wright 'a sham'); by characterising all cultural expression – such as ornament – as outmoded, or criminal, or degenerate. Yes, degenerate, culturally sick, diseased. In effect, they used the moral/evolutionary argument that became popular after Darwin and that soon Hitler was to use back at them!

The Modernists, like the sixteenth-century Protestants, were attracted by arguments of exclusion and purgation. They advocated throwing out nature (particularly the Futurists and de Stijl) and ornament (particularly Adolf Loos and Le Corbusier). The new machine civilisation was to steam-clean the environment. There is a Frank Lloyd Wright drawing, *c*1904, which he signs 'Grammar of the Protestant'. It shows his recently completed Larkin Building, by his own account a machine-age reduction to blank planes, severe lines and abstraction. The Dutch movement de Stijl (heavily indebted to Wright) opened with the proclamation of Mondrian, 'The life of contemporary cultivated man is turning gradually away from nature; it becomes more and more an a-b-s-t-r-a-c-t life.'[21]

Why? Because a mechanised culture is forcing abstraction upon us. Indeed, Mondrian's brother-in-arms, Theo van Doesberg, also with a Dutch Calvinist background (and considerably more pseudonyms than Lenin and Le Corbusier combined) took the worship of machine evolution to a preposterous level: 'Every machine is the spiritualisation of an organism.'[22]

Nature and representation were out and spiritualised mechanisms were in. So many of de Stijl's manifestos proclaim this credo, and the beginning points of their First Manifesto show why, after 1917, it became the doctrine of the new age:'1 There is an old and a new spirit of the times . . . 2 The War is destroying the old world and its contents'.[23]

Here is the final legitimisation of the Protestant Crusade; the First World War. This, according to Standard Doctrine, was caused by a civilisation thoroughly corrupt, overdecorated, smug, eclectic and class-ridden. It justified total eradication. In effect, the Protestant Crusade, aided by the machine and its flat Protestant grammar – wiped out decadence. Le Corbusier called this new age 'the vacuum cleaning period'. It stripped *beaux-arts* architecture of its corrupt decor, it cleansed the *ancien régimes* of ethnicity, it washed everything white (or at least a primary, Bauhaus colour). The crusade could only be fought as a cultural war on history, ornament, nature and the litany of Thirty Decadences – fewer than Luther's ninety-five.

The purifying function of the artist – soon made dominant in literature

[10] *Gerrit Thomas Rietveld,* **Schroeder Residence**, *Utrecht, 1924. The canonic modern building – white, abstract, overlapping planes with primary-coloured accents. 'Every machine is the spiritualisation of an organism' – with brilliant buildings like this, the Dutch Calvinists, for a short time, made one believe it. (C Jencks)*

21 Piet Mondrian, quoted from Reyner Banham, *Theory and Design in the First Machine Age*, The Architectural Press (London), 1960, p150.

22 Theo van Doesburg, ibid, p152.

23 De Stijl, ibid, p151.

and philosophy by TS Eliot and Wittgenstein – was slowly understood to be crypto-religious. As Modernism developed into Late-Modernism and further stripped itself bare, as the slogan 'less is more' became 'less than less is more than more is nearly nothing!', silence became the dominating virtue. It was a religious hush, no doubt about that; just what the mystics said – emptiness, nothingness, degree-zero. 'Whereof one cannot speak', Wittgenstein said, uttering the ultimate modernist truth, 'thereof one must be silent'. Amen.

But in the church of the avant-garde, silence can only rule for so long; most acolytes cannot hear the quiet. Thus by the 1960s, to keep the faithful in line, a new enemy had to be created. Pop Art, Neo-Dada and a host of other heresies arrived on demand, to be rooted out. By the seventies these movements grew more heads, marked radical eclecticism, pluralism, feminism and Hyperrealism; *La Pittura Colta* and *La Transavanguardia* – a Medusa-swarm of new styles and local conventions. Yet here was opportunity for more elimination – heresies are necessary for a church to survive. Furthermore, a social shift had occurred which only become apparent in the seventies. Instead of the avant-garde being a noble, oppressed minority, as it had been for one hundred and sixty years, it was – hard to believe – the reigning taste! Yes, for almost everyone, even the dreaded academy, the bourgeoisie itself. The arrière-garde? Impossible, panic, what to do? It did not fit the biblical account of good avant-garde versus diseased society. By 1980 much of the First World and its youth had been trained in Modernism, brought up in the Academies of the New. The Sunday Supplements featured de Stijl, Wright and good design; forty thousand PhDs appeared on Picasso's minor sketches and love life; Corbusieriana became a mass production industry; his 'spirit of mass production' became true in an unintended way. The new academic saints were the big three Masters of the Modern Movement, known to every student as Corb, Mies and Grope. So, when heresies grew in number, the next move of the Modern Movement came as no surprise.

THE PROTESTANT INQUISITION AMPLIFIES THE ENEMY

In October 1981, *Le Monde* announced to its morning readers, under the section of its newspaper ominously headed 'Decadence', that a spectre was haunting Europe; the spectre of Post-Modernism.[24] What Frenchmen made of this warning as they bit into their croissants is anybody's guess, especially as it came with the familiar Marxist image of a ghost looming over their civilisation (and their coffee). But they soon forgot the phantom and looked forward to the next morning's 'Decadence' column, for in our culture one ghost grows boring and must be quickly replaced by another.

The problem, however, has been that critics – especially hostile, modernist critics – will not let this one dissolve. They keep attacking the phantom with ever-increasing hysteria, making it grow into quite a substantial force that upsets not only *le petit déjeuner* but also international conferences and price quotations on the international art market. If they are not careful, there will be a panic and crash at the Museum of Modern Art as certain reputations dissolve like dead stock.

Clement Greenberg, long acknowledged as the theorist of American Modernism, defined Post-Modernism in 1979 as the antithesis of all he loved; the lowering of aesthetic standards caused by 'the democratisation of culture under industrialism'.[25] Like the 'Decadence' columnist he saw the danger as a lack of hierarchy in artistic judgement, although he did not go so far as the Frenchman in calling it simply 'nihilism'. Another art critic, Walter Darby Bannard, writing in the same prestigious *Arts Magazine* five years later, continued Greenberg's crusade against the heathens and restated the same definition, but with more brutal elaboration. 'Postmodernism', he wrote, 'is aimless, anarchic, amorphous, self-indulgent, inclusive, horizontally structured, and aims for the popular'.[26]

Given the standardised nature of these attacks, one wonders why he left out the epithets 'ruthless kitsch', or the customary comparison with Nazi populism that the architectural critic Kenneth Frampton usually adds to the list of horrors? Ever since Clement Greenberg made his famous opposition between 'Avant-Garde and Kitsch', certain intellectuals have been arguing that it has to be one thing or the other, and it is clear where they classify Post-Modernism, although of course if it is 'horizontally structured' and 'democratic' it cannot at the same time be Neo-Nazi and authoritarian. But consistency has never been a virtue of those out to malign a movement.

In the early 1980s the Royal Institute of British Architects (RIBA) hosted a series of revivalist meetings which were noteworthy for their vicious attacks

24 Gerard-Georges Lemaire, 'Le Spectre du post-modernisme', 'Decadence', *Le Monde Dimanche*, 18 October 1981, pXIV.

25 Clement Greenberg, 'Modern and Post-Modern' presented at the fourth Sir William Dobell Memorial Lecture in Sydney, Australia, on 31 October 1979 and published the following year in *Arts Magazine 54*, pp64-6.

26 Walter Darby Bannard, 'On Postmodernism', an essay originally presented at a panel on Post-Modernism at the Modern Languages Association's annual meeting in New York, 28 December 1983, published later in *Arts Magazine*.

[11] *Philip Johnson and John Burgee.* **The AT&T Building**, *New York, 1978-82. The building first branded as a Chippendale-Highboy became a monumental focus for post-modern loathing; today it seems a rather mellow New York skyscraper. (C Jencks)*

27 Aldo van Eyck, 'RPP – Rats, Posts and Other Pests', 1981 RIBA Annual Discourse published in *RIBA Journal*, *Lotus* and most fully in *AD News*, 7/81 (London) 1981, pp14-16.

28 Berthold Lubetkin, 'Royal Gold Medal Address', *RIBA*, *Transactions II*, Vol1, No2 (London) 1982, p48.

29 Berthold Lubetkin, RIBA President's Invitation Lecture, 11 June 1985, unpublished manuscript, p13. Published in part in *Building Design Magazine* (London). The comparison is with Stalin giving Corinthian columns to the people. The Prince of Wales provokes the following memory: 'I can't help recalling the diktat of Stalin fifty years ago when he said "The assumption that the specialists know better drags theory and practice into the bog of reactionary cosmopolitan opinion." The proletariat acquired the right to have their Corinthian colonnades . . .'

30 'Is Post-Modern Architecture Serious?': Paolo Portoghesi and Bruno Zevi in Conversation', *Architectural Design*, 1/2 1982, pp20-1, originally published in Italian in *L'Espresso*.

on Post-Modernism. In 1981 the Dutch architect Aldo van Eyck delivered the Annual Discourse titled 'Rats, Posts and Other Pests', and one can guess from this appellation how hard he attempted to be fair-minded. He advised his cheering audience of Modernists in a capital lettered harangue, 'Ladies and Gentlemen, I beg you, HOUND THEM DOWN AND LET THE FOXES GO' – tactics not unlike the Nazi ones he was deploring, although the hounds and foxes gave this pogrom a Wildean twist.[27] If Van Eyck advised letting the dogs loose on Post-Modernists, the older modern architect Berthold Lubetkin limited himself, on receiving his Gold Medal at the RIBA, to classifying them with homosexuals, Hitler and Stalin: 'This is a transvestite architecture, Heppelwhite and Chippendale in drag.'[28] He continued to compare Post-Modernism with Nazi kitsch in subsequent revivalist meetings in Paris and at the RIBA, even equating Prince Charles with Stalin for his attack on Modernism.[29] One could quote similar abuse from old-hat Modernists in America, Germany, Italy, France, indeed most of the world. For instance, the noted Italian critic Bruno Zevi sees Post-Modernism as a 'pastiche . . . trying to copy Classicism' and 'repressive' like fascism.[30]

We can see amid all these howls of protest something like a negative definition emerging, a paranoid definition made by Modernists in retreat, trying to hold the High Church together, issuing daily edicts denouncing heresy, keeping the faith among a confused following. It is true that through the eighties and early nineties they still kept control of most of the academies, sat on most of the aesthetic review boards, and repressed as many post-modern artists and architects as they could; but much of the creative young were not interested in suppression and the previous orthodoxy. In international competitions today the entries will be equally split between modern, post-modern, traditional and other approaches, and that generality applies as much to sculpture, painting and new forms such as performance art as it does to architecture. The door is wide open, as it was in the 1920s when Modernism had knocked down the previous academic barriers.

The irony is that today's old-time Modernists are determined to be just as paranoid as their *beaux-arts* persecutors were before them. Indeed, the slurs against Post-Modernists occasionally sound like the reactionary vitriol poured on Le Corbusier and Walter Gropius in the 1920s. Is history repeating itself? Whatever the case, these characterisations have not done what they were supposed to do – stem the tide of Post-Modernism – but, on the contrary, blown it up into a media event. Academic fury amplified the movement quickly into a brand name. Unfortunately, it also obscured the positive goals of the emergent tradition, and some of those in architecture. It is to these that we now turn.

POST-MODERNISM AS DOUBLE CODING

Post-modern movements vary in each cultural form – economics, politics, dance, psychology, education, etc – and in some areas it has not been defined or perhaps does not exist. In architecture, art, literature and philosophy – which I will look at in the next three sections – different attitudes have developed at different rates, so once again it is the pluralism and even Derrida's notion of *différance* which should be stressed (incomensurable difference). An intense commitment to pluralism is perhaps the only thing that unites every post-modern movement, and also something that marks the tradition as a Western invention, the part of the world where pluralism is most developed.

In architecture the movement grows quite independently of the word, and it has to be traced to the early 1960s and the writings of Jane Jacobs and Robert Venturi – both of whom use early ideas of complexity theory. As important is the counter culture of the 1960s, the Situationists' work in France in May 1968 and the theories of semiotics and the writings of Umberto Eco, Colin Rowe and Charles Moore. All of this questioned the hegemony of Modernism; its elitism, reductivism and exclusivism, and its anti-city and anti-history stance. By the middle seventies much of this was generally known and it was then, in 1975, that I applied the term post-modern to these various departures.[31]

In that first year of lecturing and polemicising in Europe and America, I used the term as a temporising label, as a definition to describe where we had left rather than where we were going. The observable fact was that architects as various as Ralph Erskine, Robert Venturi, Lucien Kroll, the Krier brothers and Team Ten had all departed from Modernism and set off in different directions which kept a trace of their common departure. Today I would still partly define Post-Modernism as I did in 1978 as double coding – the combination of modern techniques with something else (usually traditional building) in order for architecture to communicate with the public and a concerned minority, usually other architects. The point of this double coding was itself double. Modern architecture had failed to remain credible partly because it did not communicate effectively with its ultimate users – the main argument of my book *The Language of Post-Modern Architecture* – and partly because it did not make effective links with the city and history.

In spite of its democratic intentions, Modernism had become elitist and exclusivist. At the same time, architects, as any profession in an advanced civilisation, have to keep up with highly technical, fast-changing requirements and their professional peers. They are necessarily caught

31 My own writing and lecturing on Post-Modernism in architecture started in 1975 and 'The Rise of Post-Modern Architecture' was published in a Dutch book and a British magazine, *Architecture – Inner Town Government*, Eindhoven, July 1975, and *Architectural Association Quarterly*, No4, 1975. Subsequently Eisenman and Stern started using the term and by 1977 it had caught on. For a brief history, *see* the 'Footnote on the Term' in *The Language of Post-Modern Architecture*, fourth edition, Academy Editions, London/Rizzoli (New York), 1984, p8.

[12] Ralph Erskine, **Byker Wall**, Newcastle, 1974. Some of the first post-modern housing was ad hoc and vernacular in style making use, as here, of traditional and modern materials, green stained wood, brick, corrugated metal and asbestos. The emphasis on participation, with design acknowledging the tastes of the inhabitants, has remained a constant social goal of Post-Modernists. (C Jencks)

[13] Robert Krier, **Ritterstrasse Apartments**, Berlin-Kreuzberg, 1977-81. The white social housing of the Modernists is here adapted in a palazzo U-shaped block to form part of a perimeter block and positive urban space. Modern technology and imagery are mixed with a traditional typology, a typical double coding. This laid the foundation for IBA projects and post-modern planning in Berlin. (Gerald Blomeyer)

between society at large on the one hand and a very specialised discipline on the other. The only way out of this dilemma is a radical schizophrenia; being trained to look two opposite ways at once. Thus the solution I perceived and defined as post-modern: an architecture that was professionally based and popular as well as one that was based on new techniques and old patterns. To simplify, double coding means elite/popular, accommodating/subversive and new/old. There are compelling reasons for these opposite pairings.

First is the built-in conflict between the profession and the user of architecture, their different ways of valuing architecture, their 'codes' of perception (the science of semiotics has made this clear). Second, and stemming from this, architects must work for the power structure, society at large, and a client that may have regressive values, tastes or building motives. Wanting to build and protest at the same time, these architects, like Post-Modernists generally, send a mixed message of acceptance and critique. In a word their double coding confirms and subverts simultaneously. Third, post-modern architects were trained by Modernists, and are committed to using contemporary technology as well as facing current social reality. These commitments are enough to distinguish them from revivalists or traditionalists, a point worth stressing since it creates their hybrid language, the style of post-modern architecture. The same is not completely true of post-modern artists and writers, who may use traditional techniques of narrative and representation in a more straightforward way. Yet all the creators who could be called post-modern keep something of a modern sensibility, some intention which distinguishes their work from that of revivalists, be it irony, parody, displacement, complexity, eclecticism, realism or any number of contemporary tactics and goals. As I mentioned, Post-Modernism has the essential double meaning: the continuation of Modernism and its transcendence.

The main motivation for post-modern architecture is obviously the social failure of modern architecture, its mythical 'death' announced repeatedly over ten years. In 1968, an English tower block of housing, Ronan Point, suffered 'cumulative collapse' as its floors gave way after an explosion. In 1972, many slab blocks of housing were intentionally blown up at Pruitt-Igoe in St Louis. By the mid-seventies, these explosions were becoming a quite frequent method of dealing with the failures of modernist building methods: cheap prefabrication, lack of personal 'defensible' space and the alienating housing estate. The 'death' of modern architecture and its ideology of progress, which offered technical solutions to social problems, was seen by everyone in a vivid way.

The idea that modernity could die is quite sophisticated, or at least intuitively complex, because it means comprehending that the ideology of being 'just now', living exclusively in the present tense, can expire. Before the collapse of Communism (perhaps modernity's greatest construction) in 1989, there were few indications on a popular level that the modern world view and its practice were coming to an end. In reality, the dramatic failures of modern housing had political and social implications far beyond architecture; they were a harbinger of later catastrophes to come – Chernobyl; Black Monday 1987, when five trillion dollars vanished from the global economy; the Exxon/Valdez oil spill, the deathly leak of chemicals at Bhopal; the hole in the ozone layer and other growing ecological threats. In addition, the modernist destruction of the central city was almost as apparent to the populace as the failure of housing estates. Social realities should be stressed in architecture because they are not quite the same in other fields. There is no vivid 'death' of Modernism in art or literature, nor the same social motivation that one finds in post-modern architecture.

Yet even in post-modern literature there is a social motive for using past forms in an ironic way. Umberto Eco has given a classic formulation of this irony or double coding:

> I think of the postmodern attitude as that of a man who loves a very cultivated woman and knows he cannot say to her, 'I love you madly', because he knows that she knows (and that she knows that he knows) that these words have already been written by Barbara Cartland. Still, there is a solution. He can say, 'As Barbara Cartland would put it, I love you madly'. At this point, having avoided false innocence, having said clearly that it is no longer possible to speak innocently, he will nevertheless have said what he wanted to say to the woman: that he loves her; but he loves her in an age of lost innocence. If the woman goes along with this, she will have received a declaration of love all the same. Neither of the two speakers will feel innocent, both will have accepted the challenge of the past, of the already said which cannot be eliminated; both will consciously and with pleasure play the game of irony . . . But both will have succeeded, once again, in speaking of love.[32]

Thus Eco underlines the lover's use of post-modern double coding and extends it to the novelist's and poet's social use of previous forms. We cannot avoid 'the already said'; both the past and our difference from it. Futurists and Modernists declared a war on memory and this led, ultimately, to silence and the void. What else can one do, if memory is banished, but shut up? Opposed to this late-modern quiescence John Barth (1980) and

[14] Berthold Lubetkin and Tecton, **Hallfield Estate Housing**, London, 1947-55. The typology of Le Corbusier's 'City in the Park' led to an urbanism which was first criticised by Jane Jacobs in 1961 and then later by a chorus of writers including Robert Goodman, Oscar Newman, Rob Krier, Colin Ward and, recently, Alice Coleman. Lack of personal 'defensible space' represents just one of the problems of this typology; scale, density and symbolism are equally questionable. (C Jencks)

32 Umberto Eco, *Postscript to The Name of the Rose*, Harcourt Brace Jovanovich (New York and London), 1984, pp67-8.

[15] James Stirling, Michael Wilford and Associates, **Neue Staatsgalerie**, *Stuttgart, 1977-84. 'Ruins in the Garden', classical blocks which have fallen about in an eighteenth-century manner, reveal the reality of post-modern construction: a steel frame holds up the slabs of masonry, and there is no cement between the blocks, but rather air. Elegant black voids, ironic vents to the garage, dramatise truth and illusion. (C Jencks)*

[16] **Neue Staatsgalerie**. *The sculpture court, a transformation of the Pantheon and Hadrian's Villa among other classical types, is a true* res publica *with the public brought through the site on a curvilinear walkway to the right. Traditional and modern 'language games' are not synthesised but juxtaposed, an allegory of a schizophrenic culture. (C Jencks)*

[17] **Neue Staatsgalerie**. *The 'Acropolis' perched on a garage shows further aspects of the discontinuous pluralism which Jean-François Lyotard and others see as a defining aspect of Post-Modernism. Oddly, the role of ornament is taken on by modernist forms and function by traditional ones. This ironic reversal of twentieth-century convention implies a new set of standards which throws in doubt both Neo-Classical and modern aesthetics. (C Jencks)*

33 Linda Hutcheon, *A Poetics of Postmodernism, History, Theory, Fiction*, Routledge (New York/London), 1988, pp3-22.

34 *See* John Barth, 'The Literature of Replenishment, Postmodernist Fiction', *The Atlantic*, January 1980, pp65-71, and Umberto Eco, 'Postmodernism. Irony. The Enjoyable', *Postscript to the Name of the Rose*, Harcourt Brace Jovanovich, (New York and London), 1984, first published in Italian, 1983.

Umberto Eco (1983) defined a postmodern literature which used the full panoply of literary means. Their own novels – Eco's *The Name of the Rose* is typical – cut across literary genres and combined such separated types as the historical romance, comedy, detective story, and philosophical treatise. Again, Post-Modernism always carries the injunction to cross territories, break down modernist specialisation, hybridise discourses, attack false boundaries. As Linda Hutcheon has so exhaustively shown, postmodern fiction inscribes itself within conventional discourses in order to subvert them. It incorporates cultural realities in order to challenge them: a double coding as strategy.[33]

John Barth sees the postmodern as a search for a wider audience, yet one that does not deny the real insights of Modernity:

My ideal postmodernist author neither merely repudiates nor merely imitates either his twentieth-century modernist parents or his nineteenth-century premodernist grandparents. He has the first half of our century under his belt, but not on his back. Without lapsing into moral or artistic simplicity, shoddy craftsmanship, Madison Avenue venality, or either false or real naiveté he nevertheless aspires to a fiction more democratic in its appeal than such late-modernist marvels (by my definition and in my judgement) as Beckett's *Stories and Texts for Nothing* or Nabokov's *Pale Fire*. He may not hope to reach and move the devotees of James Michener and Irving Wallace – not to mention the lobotomised mass-media illiterates. But he should hope to reach and delight, at least part of the time, beyond the circle of what Mann used to call the Early Christians: professional devotees of high art.[34]

The injunction goes beyond the restricted audience of the Early Christians without sacrificing quality or the valid insights of Modernists such as Darwin, Marx and Freud. Faced with an exclusivist Modernism, a minimalism of means and ends, Barth and other writers have felt just as hemmed in as architects forced to build in the International Style, or using only glass and steel.

The most notable and convincing use of this double coding in architecture is James Stirling's addition to the Staatsgalerie in Stuttgart. Here one can find the fabric of the city and the existing museum extended in amusing and ironic ways. The U-shaped *palazzo* form of the old gallery is echoed and placed on a high plinth, or 'Acropolis', above the traffic. But this classical base holds a very real and necessary parking garage, one that is indicated ironically by stones which have 'fallen', like ruins, to the ground. The resultant holes show the real construction – not the thick marble blocks [of the real Acropolis, but a steel frame holding stone cladding which allows the air ventilation required by law. One can sit on these false ruins and

ponder the truth of our lost innocence; that we live in an age which can build with beautiful, expressive masonry as long as we make it skin-deep and hang it on a steel skeleton. A Modernist would of course deny himself and us this pleasure for a number of reasons: 'truth to materials', 'logical consistency', and the ever present drive to purge and purify.

By contrast Stirling, like the lovers of Umberto Eco, wants to communicate more and different values. To signify the permanent nature of the museum, he has used traditional rustication and classical forms including an Egyptian cornice, an open-air Pantheon, and segmental arches. These are beautiful [in an understated and conventional way, though they are not revivalist either, because of small distortions, or the use of a modern material such as reinforced concrete. They say: 'We are beautiful like the Acropolis or Pantheon, but we are also based on concrete technology and deceit.' The extreme form of this double coding is visible at the entry points, a steel temple outline which announces the drop-off point and the modernist steel canopies which indicate the entrance to the public. These forms and colours are reminiscent of de Stijl – that quintessentially modern language – but they are collaged onto the traditional background. Thus Modernism confronts Classicism to such an extent that both Modernists and Classicists would be surprised, if not offended. There is not the simple harmony and consistency of either language or world view. In effect Stirling is saying that we live in a complex world where we cannot deny either the past and conventional beauty, or the present and current technical and social reality. Caught between this past and present, unwilling to oversimplify our situation, Stirling has produced the most 'real' beauty of post-modern architecture to date.

This reality has as much to do with taste as it does with technology. Modernism failed as mass-housing and city building partly because it failed to communicate with its users, who might not have liked the style, understood what it meant or even known how to use it. Therefore double coding, (the essential definition of Post-Modernism), has been adopted as a strategy for communicating on various levels at once. Virtually every post-modern architect – Robert Venturi, Hans Hollein, Charles Moore, Aldo Rossi, Frank Gehry, Arata Isozaki are the notable examples – use popular and elitist signs in their work to achieve quite opposite ends. Their styles are essentially hybrid. To simplify, at Stuttgart the blue and red handrails and vibrant polychromy fit in with the youth that uses the museum. They resemble their dayglo hair and anoraks while the Classicism [appeals more to the lovers of Schinkel. This is a very popular building with young and old, and when I interviewed people there – a group of *plein air* painters, schoolchildren and businessmen – I found their different perceptions and tastes were accommodated and stretched. The pluralism which is so often called on to justify Post-Modernism is here a tangible reality.

This is not the place to recount in detail the history of post-modern architecture, but I want to stress the ideological and social intentions which underlie this history because they are completely denied by the Protestant Inquisition.[35] Even traditionalists often reduce the debate to matters of style, and thus the symbolic intentions and morality are overlooked. If one reads the writings of Robert Venturi, Denise Scott Brown, Christian Norberg-Schulz, or mine, one will find the constant notion of pluralism: the idea that the architect must design for different 'taste cultures' (in the words of the sociologist Herbert Gans) and for differing views of the good life. In any complex building, in any large city building such as an office, there will be varying tastes and functions that have to be articulated and these will inevitably lead, if the architect follows these hints, towards a radical eclecticism. He may pull this heterogeneity together under a Free-Style Classicism, as does Stirling, or a more unified method of 'folding in difference', as does Peter Eisenman, but a trace of the pluralism will and should remain.[36]

There are, inevitably, many more strands of post-modern architecture than the radical eclecticism and urbanism I have discussed, and in the evolutionary tree overleaf, I have represented six basic traditions. There is some overlap between these identifiable 'species' and architects, unlike animal species, can jump from one category to another, or occupy several strands at once. The diagram also shows two fundamental aspects which have to be added to the previous definition of post-modern architecture. First, it is a movement that starts roughly in 1960 after the High Modernism of the 1920s lost its direction and, second, it is a set of plural departures from Modernism. Thus, key definers are pluralism and a critical relation to a pre-existing ideology.

It is an academic but important point that, if one is going to classify anything as complex as an architectural movement, one has to use many definers. In a key text on Baroque and Rococo, Anthony Blunt shows the necessity for using ten definers;[37] in distinguishing Post-Modernism from modern and late-modern architecture, I have used thirty. Some of these are most noticeable to the public; the new presence of wit, ornament, polychromy and metaphor – things banished by the Modernists. Others are less visible and concern symbolism, expressive technology, a new ambiguous space, urban contextualism and the relation of the architect to existing and past cultures.

[18] *Peter Eisenman,* **Max Reinhardt Haus***, project for Berlin, 1993. Folding in difference became a non-conflictual way of handling heterogeneity. For this project a skyscraper, omnicentre, triumphal arch and various conflicting city functions are resolved under a fractal set of self-similar forms.*

[19] **Evolutionary Tree of Post-Modern Architecture, 1960-1990**. *In any major movement there are various strands running concurrently which have to be distinguished because of differing values. Here the six main traditions of Post-Modernism show their common ground and differences and illustrate the fact that, since the late 1970s, Post-Modern Classicism and urbanism have been unifying forces.*

35 My own main writings on the subject are *The Language of Post-Modern Architecture*, sixth edition, Academy Editions (London), 1991 and *Architecture Today*, Academy Editions (London), 1982 and Rizzoli (New York), 1982, 1988 and *Modern Movements in Architecture*, second edition, Penguin Books (Harmondsworth), 1985. *See also* Paolo Portoghesi, *After Modern Architecture*, Rizzoli (New York), 1982, and its updated version, *Postmodern*, Rizzoli (New York), 1983, and *Immagini del Post-Moderno*, Edizioni Chiva, (Venice), 1983. *See also* Heinrich Klotz, *Die Revision der Moderne, Postmoderne Architektur, 1960-1980* and *Moderne und Postmoderne Architektur der Gegenwart 1960-1980*, Friedr Vieweg & Sohn (Braunschweig/ Wiesbaden), 1984. We have debated his notion of post-modern architecture as 'fiction' and this has been published in *Architectural Design* 7/8 1984, 'Revision of the Modern'. *See also* my discussion of users and abusers of post-modern in 'La Bataille des etiquettes', *Nouveau plaisirs d'architecture*, Centre Georges Pompidou (Paris), 1985, pp25-33.

36 *See* 'Folding in Architecture', *Architectural Design*, 3/4, 1993, Profile 102.

37 Anthony Blunt, *Some Uses and Misuses of the Terms Baroque and Rococo as applied to Architecture* (Oxford), 1973; Charles Jencks, *Late-Modern Architecture*, Academy Editions (London), 1980 and Rizzoli (New York) 1980, p32.

1960   **1965**   **1970**

HISTORICISM

RUDOLPH - Jewett Cente
- Wellesley Coll
VENTURI - N Penn Nurses HQ
- Venturi Hse
- *Complexity and Contradiction*
REGIONALISM
Learning from Las Vegas
VENTURI SCHOOL
HHP - Hadley Hse   GIURGOLA - Sherman Fairchi
BROOKS - Btwth   SCULLY
NEO - SHINGLE STYLE
BOFILL - Meritxell - Arcades du Lac

FORMALISM
SAARINEN
JOHNSON - Dumbarton Oaks
YAMASAKI
NEO - LIBERTY
GARDELLA   ALBINI   BARDESCHI
AULENTI   BARCELONA SCHOOL
MORETTI   CORREA   MBM
NEO-STYLES
CLOTET & TUSQUETS   **RADICAL ECLECT**
DRAWING   KOOLHAAS
PORTOGHESI - Casa Papanice   GLENDENN
- Islamic Centre
JOWSEY   REICHLIN + REINHART - Maison
OUTRAM   ZO ATELIER
GOWAN
PORTOGHESI
JAPAN STYLE
MAEKAWA   KIKUTAKE   GRAU
TANGE   KUROKAWA

ORNA

STRAIGHT REVIVALISM

DISNEYLAND   LAPIDUS   REHABILI
Madonna Inn   GRADIGE
PUERTO BANUS
PORTMEIRION

WAR REBUILDING - WARSAW   REED   PASTICHE   SPOERRY - Port Grimaud
ERITH   **BOLOGNA**

TRUE VERNACULAR - FATHY   LA POP   GAY ELECT
INTERIOR DECORATION
HICKS
BENNISO

NEO-VERNACULAR

DARBOURNE & DARK - Pimlico   ABK - Chichester Coll   VENTURI - Trubek & Wislocki Hses
- Islington   MAGUIRE & MURRAY   - Franklin Ct   BOLOGN
- Pershore
STOUT & LITCHFIELD   MOORE - Sea Ranch   MINSTER LOVEL

REGIONALISM   GLENDENNING
ESHERICK
KUMP - Foothill Coll   GUEDES
BARNES - Haystack Mountain School
- St Pauls School   **INSTANT COMMUNITIES**

MBM   ERSKINE   RECYCLING
'LOST NEW YORK'
PORT GRIMAUD

AD-HOC URBANIST

JOHANSEN - Mummers Theater
- Johansen Hse
TAKEYAMA - Housing
GOFF - Price Hse   GREENE   SELLERS - Goddard Coll   **ADHOCISM**   ERSKINE - Byker
- Gryder Hse   GUEDES   HANDMADE HOUSES   WAMPER
DROP CITY   SELF-BUILT   TURNER
TOWNSCAPE   ROSSI - *L'Architettura della citta*
ARAU
GOODMAN   **CONTEXTUALISM**   R KRIER - Morph
BOFILL - Calle JS Bach   L KRIER - Echternach   - Stuttg
- S Greg   URBAN PROTEST   - Royal Mint Sq   - Ritters
- Barrio Gaudi   Covent Garden   DE FEO   - La Villete   GREGOTTI
- Xanadu   Les Halles   - Luxembourg
UNGERS - Student Hostel   AMSTERDAM   - Nolli's Rome
COLLINS - 'Sitte Revival'   - Tiergarten Museum   BRUSSELS
- Marburg   AYMONINO   PINON

METAPHOR METAPHYSICAL

LEO   ISHIYAMA - Fantasy Villa
GOFF - Nicol Hse   ISOZAKI - Fuji
UTZON   TAKEYAMA - Pepsi Plant   HARA - Hara Hse
Sydney Opera House   PIETILA   - Beverly Tom hotel   - Awazu Hse
RONCHAMP   MIYAWAKI - Blue Box Hse
SEMIOTICS   - Akita Sogo Bank   AIDA - Nirvana Hse
PORRO   - Hse like a die
TWA Terminal   **ANTHROPOMORPHISM**   - Stepped-Platform
MEANING IN ARCHITECTURE   'Blue Whale'   HOWARD
AULENTI   ARQUITECTONICA
BARRAGAN   NORBERG - SCHULZ   PICHLER   SHIRAI   RANALLI
COATE

POST-MODERN SPACE

SKEWS, DIAGONALS   NETSCH   MICHELS
JOHANSEN   **SUPERGRAPHICS**
VENTURI - N Penn Nurses HQ   WALKER
- Venturi Hse   **MOORE** - Aedicules   TURNBULL - Zimmermann Hse
- Brant Hse   REVERSE PERSPECTIVE   - Moore Hse   HHP
AALTO - Saynatsalo Town Hall   KAHN - Wrap around ruins   - Sea Ranch   STERN - Bourke Hse Poolhse
- Imatra   - Goldberg Hse   - Santa Barbara   - Westchester Res
SCHAROUN - Berlin Phil.   - Salk Lab   - Klotz Hse   **DEMI - FORMS + SURPRIS**
- Stern Hse
LE CORBUSIER - Carpenter Centre   - Rudolph Hse   POSITIVE/NEGATIVE REVI
'Hadrian's Villa'   PASANELLA - Dunbar Hse   **FRONTALITY/ROTATION**   **LAYERING +**
- Grau Hse   GRAVES - Hanselmann Hse   **AMBIG**
MEIER - Smith Hse   - Gunwyn Ventures
- Douglas Hse   EISENMAN - Houses I-XI
HEJDUK - Diamond Series

JOHNSON - AT&T Building
VENTURI - Trubek & Wislocki Hses
MOORE - Xanadune
- Kresge Coll
- Piazza d'Italia
COHEN
PRAN

- Franklin Ct
- 'Signs of Life' **FRIDAY**
- Brant Hse HHT Washington
- Morris HQ **BEEBY** - Townhouse
Shirai

Ferri
- Blum Res
Jan - Jon

Farrell
- Clifton
- TVAM
- Henley Regatta
- Fenchurch St
- Portzamparc
- Conservatoire

VENTURI
- Gordon Wu
- Long Island Hse
Ishii
- Gable Blg
Ambasz
- 'fables'
- Banque Lambert

Gough Gund
Correa
Clelland - Goa Hotel

KLOTZ

- DAM
Shin Toki + Tange
- Tsukuba Mun Gym

TG SMITH - Doric Hse
- Matthews St Hse
- Long Hse

HOLLEIN - Perchtoldsdorf
- Tehran Museum
- Travel Bureaux

DIXON - St Marks Rd
MOZUNA
TAFT

FINLAY
- Writings
- Garden

DIXON
- Lanark Rd
- Opera Hse

JENCKS
- LPMA
- PMC
- TSA
- Thematic Hse

SYMBOLIC ARCHITECTURE
Kajima

Kurokawa
Hiroshima MOMA

MOZUNA
- Kushiro Mus
Murano

Heimsath
- Kagan Chaple

JOURDAN / PAS
- Frankfurt Bank
- Hotel Hohenhaus

GRAVES - Schulman Hse
- Crooks Hse
- Kalko Hse
- Fargo Hse
- Sunar Showroom
- Portland Building

T WATANABE - Nakauchi Hse
TIGERMAN - Apartments

HOLLEIN
- Schullin II
- Mönchengladbach
- Frankfurt Mus
- Berlin Scheme

SITE
Haas Hse
Allsteel

STERN
- Cohn Pool
- Point West
- Bozzi
- Lawson
- UVA

BEEBY
- Synagogue
- Library
- Pediatrics

Taft
- Rivercrest C.C.
Von Branca
Nunez-Yanowsky
- Picasso Arena

OUTRAM
- Isle of Dogs
- Rausing Hse

VENTURI
- National Gallery Ext
AULENTI
- Musee d'Orasay

POST-MODERN CLASSICISM

EXHIBITIONS
M.JOHNSON - Ovenden Hse
UTYENS REVIVAL HIGUERAS - Ciudad Real City Hall
UX-BEAUX-ARTS EXHIBITION KIJIMA - Matsuo Shrine
GREENBERG - Courthouse STERN - Jerome Greene Hall
- House - McGarry/Appignani Bedroom
cy Museum - X Residence

PORTOGHESI
- Venice Biennale
- La Banca Populare
- L'Aquila

GRAVES
- San Juan Library
- Humana
- Clos Pegase
- Whitney

KOHN PEDERSEN FOX
- 333 Wacker
- Hercules
- Proctor + Gamble
- 180 E 70
- Hyatt Reg Hotel

REGIONALIST ROMANTICISM
VANDENHOVE **TALLER BOFILL**
- Delforge Hse - Arcades
- Blanche Hse - Abraxas
- Hors-Chateau - Montpelier
- Cergy-Pontoise
- XIV Arrondissement

PATTERN BOOKS
JAMESON CASSON - Plunkett
TERRY - Country Houses
- Mosque

Kahn
- Dacca Ass

LEON KRIER
- Berlin-Tegel
- Pliny's Villa
- Completion of Washington
TERRY
- Waverton
- RIVERSIDE
Tigerman
- Anti-Cruelty
Doring
Urabe
Gasson
- Burrell

Moore, Ruble, Yudell
- St Matthew's
Hoover Berg Desmond
- Douglas County Admin

PELLI
- Pier 4

ISOZAKI
- Tsukuba
- MOCA
- Graphic Museum

Mather
- Climatic Rsh SOM
- Rowes Whf
- 200 Ross

POST-MODERN CLASSICISM
COBB
- Portland Mus

EL-WAKIL
- Island Mosque Jeddar
- Al Sulaiman Palace

Buffi
- Cergy
- National Art School

Colquhoun + Miller
- Whitechaple
Hiroshi Oe
- National Noh Theatre

Purini + Thermes
Holl
Ungers + Kiss
- Hobbs Res

CULLINAN - Leighton Creasent
DERBYSHIRE - Hillingdon Centre
SHER & FRIEDMAN

ARQUITECTONICA - Miami Hse
- Skyscrapers

REHABILITATION
LDEN & MAWSON JOURDAN
VAN EYCK - Zwolle Housing
- Hubertus Home
BOUT & LEY

DIXON - St Mark's Rd
ISHII
GLC POLICY

VERNACULAR CLASSICISM
Aga Khan Awards Boccara
MIMAR Kamal El-Kafrawi
JONES - Qatar Univ
- Mississauga City Hall Garay

Roca
- S Vincente Market
BDM
- Costa Brava Hse
Lion
MYERS
- Phonix Comp

MOORE - Church Street S Hsing
- Kresge Coll.
KROLL - Louvain Univ R WALKER - Houses

BLOM

R KRIER + KLEIHUES
- IBA Berlin

Neumann **NORDIC CLASSICISM**
Bofinger

CONSTRUCTIVIST CLASSICISM
Porphyrios - Classicism is not a style

Linazorno
Iniquez + Ustarroz

DUANY + PLATER-ZYBERK
- Seaside
- Vilanova House

RRATIONALISM
MA ROWE - Collage City

GRAU
MISSING LINK
PORPHYRIOS
COSENTINO

MOHL
- Karlsruhe Bank

STIRLING
- Clore
- Harvard
- Mansion House
- STUTTGART
- Berlin

AIDA
- Toy Block Houses

Anselmi Grassi
- Slaughterhouse

HILMER + SATTLER
- Haus Fetzer Herrlich

NATALINI
- Computer Ctr Bank

KLIMENT + HALSBAND
David Lloyd Jones
- National Farmer's Union

HUET KLEIHUES
BLOMEYER

STIRLING - Dusseldorf Museum
- Meineke Strasse
- Staatsgalerie Stuttgart
- Harvard Museum
- Columbia Univ

Kahn Revival

BOTTA
- Massagno Hse
- Viganello Hse
- Origlio Hse
- Offices

SHIN TOKI
Tsukuba Municipal Gym
Community Architecture
- Prince Charles' speech
- Rod Hackney

ITO
- Watanabe
- Houses
TAKEYAMA
- Nakamura Hosp

A TENDENZA
NEO-RATIONALISM
ROSSI - Gallaratese
- Modena Cemetery
- Fagnano Olona School
- Teatro del Mondo
BENAMO & PORTZAMPARC - Rue des Hautes Formes
CIRIANI - Housing MONTES - Cergy - Pontoise

BOFILL - Arcades du Lac
BOTTA - Morbio School

ROSSI MONEO
- Il Teatro - Museum
- Berlin
- Casa Aurora
- Studio works
- Southside
BATEY + MACK
- Holt Hse

UNGERS
- Frankfurt Fair
- Frankfurt Tower
- ARCH AS THEME
- Bremerhaven
- Dam
Culot
- Exhibitions

CAMPI Hershman
- Casa Pollini - Giloh Quarter Hsg
- Casa Maggi

URBANIST CLASSICISM
ROBERTSON Cullinan
- Houses - New Court
- Washington Offices
ARGEST + GANDELSONAS
- Urban Fragments

Vacchini
- Casa Maria

ALEXANDER
- PATTERN LANGUAGE
- NEW EISHIN CAMPUS

PORTOGHESI
Vallo di Diano
- Mariessehof Hsg

ERMAN - Hot Dog Hse
- Daisy Hse
- Animal Crackers
- Best Home of All
- Heaven Phase

ITO - PMT Building
BOTTA - Houses
ISHII - 54 Windows
- Naoshima

Kroll
- Alma Metro Station

Rokkaku
- Kouko Ch

Tremaglio
- Arena Hse
Jourdan et al
- Frankfurt Bank
Berghof Landesbank

Crepain
- Hsg over shops

PELLI
- Four Leaf Tower

TAKAMATSU

ANTHROPOMORPHIC
Hunziker
- Les Grottes, Geneva

MOZUNA
- Zen Temple
- Yosue Hse
ARI
ABRAHAM
FACE HOUSES
FERRI
AGREST WILSON
CHADO GOUGH
SILVETTI MACK

SITE - Peeling Project
- Indeterminate Facade
- Notch Project
YAMASHITA - Face Hse
- Dental Clinic
OMA - Delirious New York - Tokeo Office
- Hotel Spinx
VENTURI - Brant Johnson Hse
BOFILL - Monuments

TEAM ZOO
- Domo con Kula
- 2nd Hand Car Dealer
GHIYAMA + SUZUKI
- Sunflower
- Chohachi Arts Mus
- Egg Dome
- Farmers Hse

Tigerman
- Pompadour
Kijima + YAS
- The Ch of Saint Domes

HUMOUR

PIETILA
- Herranta Market
- Sief Palace
- Lieska Ch

ROMANTIC FOLK REVIVAL
Ranko Radovic
- Nago City Hall
- Shinshkan
HIROSHI HARA
- Yamato International HQ
CSETE + DULANSKI
- Cave Rsch

MAKOVECZ - Mortuary Hall
- Sarospatak Cultural Centre
- Ski Lodge

ALBERTS
NMB Bank HQ

SYMMETRICAL SYMMETRY
GRAVES - Mezzo Hse
- Crooks Hse
- Warehouse conversion
- Kalko Hse
- Plocek Hse

ASPLUND REVIVAL - Villa Snellman
VENTURI - Brant Hse
MOORE - Burnes Hse
- Dental Clinic
- Tokyo Office

Corrigan
Van Hoy + Elian
- Springwood Drive

Jan + Jon
- Oslo Univ Press
- Skogbrand

Nouvel
- Belfort Theatre

DISSONANT COLLAGE
Moss
- 708 Hse
- Petal Hse

COATE - Alexander Hse
'Hotle matignon' 'La Malgrange'
PELLI - Pacific Design Centre
FUJII - Houses
MOZUNA - Anti-Dwelling Box
- Yin-Yang Hse

SHIFTED AXES
TG SMITH - Matthews Street Hse
- Long Hse
KUPPER - Nilsson Hse

GEHRY - Gehry Hse

MEIER - Atheneum

GEHRY
- Loyola
- Aerospace
- Wosk
- Winton

MORPHOSIS
- Houses

MOORE RUBLE YUDELL
- Kwee Hse
Holzbauer
- Hse for Art Collector

*[20] Venice Biennale, **Strada Novissima**, 1980. Visible facades are by Venturi, Rauch and Scott Brown and Leon Krier. The Strada illustrates the 'return to architecture', to polychromy, ornament and, above all, to the notion of the street as an urban type.*

[21] Arata Isozaki, Tsukuba Civic Centre, Japan, 1980-3. Ledoux and Michaelangelo, absorbed in Free-Style Classicism, rendered in High-Tech. (Satoru Mishima)

THE COUNTER-REFORMATION IN ARCHITECTURE

In 1927, at the well-publicised exhibition in Stuttgart called the Weissenhof Settlement, the white International Style and the Machine Aesthetic became unofficial modernist dogma. Official modernist dogma says that there are no dogmas, but the exhibition proved otherwise and everyone got the point. By 1927 it was no secret which sins were to be extirpated – criminal ornament, ruling-class historicism, degenerate classicism – and which virtues were to extol function, abstraction, machines, machines, machines.

Fifty-three years later, in the old Arsenale in Venice, all this transvaluation was itself transvalued. Paolo Portoghesi, other critics, architects and I, organised the Biennale of Architecture around the theme 'The Presence of the Past'. Back were ornament, symbolism and a few other taboos. The Strada Novissima, based on a Renaissance stage-set, consisted of twenty facades designed by leading post-modern architects. Most of them were in a Free-Style Classicism, a style which used the full repertoire of mouldings, keystones and columnar orders, but usually in an ironic fashion, indicating their place in history after Modernism, acknowledging that the return to tradition had to be based on current social and technical realities. Since then the most challenging post-modern Classicism has grown in strength to be practised around the world – even by the Indians and Japanese – using materials such as prefabricated concrete and aluminium.

The Counter-Reformation also needed missionaries, to establish its renewed orthodoxy. Aldo Rossi, an Italian Pope of architecture, issued decrees on Neo-Rationalism and the importance of memory for rebuilding the city (destroyed by Modernism). The idea of autonomous architecture returned, an architecture responding to its own typological laws of streets, squares and city blocks. In encyclical after encyclical, the monument, which Modernists declared forbidden, was reinstated. The most militant apostle, Leon Krier, a veritable Ignatius Loyola, established his own following called Rational Architects, equivalent to the Society of Jesus. And these New Jesuits from Spain, Italy, Belgium and France often insisted on building with ancient techniques of craftsmanship and stone. An indication of how powerful St Ignatius Krier became, even without building a single structure, is that in 1985 he was given a grand exhibition of drawings in the High Church of Modernism, the Museum of Modern Art.

The doctrines spread very quickly, with exhibitions in Helsinki, Chicago and Tokyo. A northern Vatican was established in Frankfurt where Heinrich Klotz made a thorough collection of post-modern documents, drawings and models in a building which could be called the first museum of

2] post-modern architecture (specially designed by Matthias Ungers). If the 1927 Weissenhof exhibition represents the public triumph of Protestantism, then the 1980 Venice Biennale and its subsequent resurrections in Paris and San Francisco represent the triumph of the Counter-Reformation and its several Councils of Trent.

Before I drop this parable, a last parallel should be mentioned. The real Counter-Reformation resulted in the Baroque style (then called the Jesuit Style) and the building of many splendid churches replete with exuberant polychromy and narrative sculpture. All this was a sign of a new spirituality and the new authority of the Church. While the stylistic parallel of the Counter-Reformation with Post-Modernism can be made – and there is even a New Baroque – there is no single faith to give it substance. Rather, there is the plural post-modern agenda and the new metanarrative which has emerged with the post-modern sciences of complexity: cosmogenesis, the universe story. This started what I see as the second phase of Post-Modernism, which we will return to in conclusion after looking at other shifts from Modernism. But, to summarise the first phase, we can point to certain attainments which became generalised in much of the dominant culture.

By the mid-eighties, the notion of contextual city rebuilding had become widely accepted to replace the total urban renewal, or the *tabula rasa* approach, of the Modernists. Three urban interventions stand out. The great city plan of San Francisco was passed in 1986 mandating many of Jane Jacobs' ideas, including mixed development and legislation controlling the car. Throughout the eighties West Berlin was rebuilt under the guidance of an institute known as IBA, which adopted all sorts of post-modern strategies including perimeter block planning and figure/ground composition, where the public space became the figure and the private realm the background. Barcelona, under its self-styled post-modern mayor Pasqual Maragall, became an exemplary model of pluralist planning, with different treatment of the city's

3] sectors, creation of over a hundred parks, enhancement of the each district's peculiar qualities and new building to complete the nineteenth-century plan.

By 1990, history, symbolism, narrative, pluralism, the role of memory, place, and local culture had been accepted as worthy of support, even by Modernists. By contrast, the notions of double coding, and resisting consumerism while acknowledging it, remain more controversial and confined to the post-modern tradition. Most generally accepted with critical acclaim were the exemplary buildings of James Stirling, Robert Venturi, Aldo Rossi, Hans Hollein, Kisho Kurokawa and Arata Isozaki. Characteristically, they cut across taste cultures and time, they referred to past, present and future as an evolutionary chain, and they challenged categories of exclusion.

[22] OM Ungers, **German Architectural Museum**, Frankfurt, 1982-4, heralded as the Museum of post-modern architecture on account of its white gridded abstraction along with the collection of drawings, plans and models built up by Heinrich Klotz. (C Jencks)

[23] Beverly Pepper, **Landscape**, Parc de l'Estacio del Nord, Barcelona, Spain, 1991. The decentralisation of Barcelona into districts and many parks was a post-modern policy of renewal brought in by Mayor Pasqual Maragall. (C Jencks)

[24] Eric Owen Moss, **Hayden Tract**, Culver City, LA, 1993-4. A multiple-voice discourse of old building and new fabric, dome and skylight, stair and wall, abstraction and representation (note the head with hat – logo for the owner). Post-Modernism in the nineties. (C Jencks)

38 For my critiques of post-modern kitsch *see* 'Post-Modernism on Trial', *Architectural Design*, 1991 and *The Language of Post-Modern Architecture*, sixth edition, Academy Editions (London), 1991, last chapter.

These were the attainments of architectural and urban Post-Modernism.

However, the media success of the movement, coupled with the building boom of the eighties, led to an inevitable excess, particularly on a commercial level. Even among more serious architects there was confusion and loss of direction as they became commercially successful and as overworked as Modernists in their heyday. In 1985, at the height of his Po-Mo period, Philip Johnson had two and a half billion dollars worth of work. This inflationary period is typified by the rather kitsch work of Michael Graves for the Disney Corporation. Post-Modernism, like the corporate Modernism of the 1960s, was loathed for this ersatz and inflation – and understandably so.[38] The degeneracy which Modernists predicted came true, but not for the reasons they gave (rather the consumerism, success and industrial replication which have destroyed every living movement since 1800 naturally took their toll). Po-Mo, to put it in theoretical terms, is like Mo-Mo, and Late-Mo – just another entropic vulgarisation caused by mass culture. Everything creative and exemplary ends as junk. Rare is the successful school which is not corrupted in five years; extremely rare is the tradition which keeps creatively sharp for ten.

Thus, by the late 1980s, the second stage of Post-Modernism reacted to the first, and resulted in small-block planning, ambiguity, understatement, and a heterogeneous language of architecture. Some of the work of Frank Gehry, Eric Owen Moss, Daniel Libeskind and Peter Eisenman typifies this next period. It refers to history, but not so directly; it is eclectic but in an understated way; it acknowledges the validity of symbolism, ornament, the media, the perennial themes of architecture, but in an oblique way. In spite of this ambiguity it is still a vital part of the Counter-Reformation; it resists the puritan reduction of architecture to function, abstraction and machine imagery.

POST-MODERN ART – SUBVERTING WHILE INSCRIBING

Like post-modern architecture, the art movement also began c1960 with a succession of departures from Modernism; notably, Pop Art, Hyper-realism, Photo Realism, Allegorical and Political Realism, New Image Painting, La Transavanguardia, Neo-Expressionism and a host of other more or less fabricated movements. Pressure from the art market to produce new labels and synthetic schools no doubt increased the tempo and heat of this change. The influence of the international media, so emphasised as a defining aspect of the post-industrial society, has caused these movements to cross over national boundaries.

Post-modern art, like architecture, is influenced by the global network and the sensibility that comes with this – an ironic cosmopolitanism. If one looks at three Italian Post-Modernists, Carlo Maria Mariani, Sandro Chia and Mimmo Paladino, one sees their 'Italianness' always in quotation marks, an ironic fabrication of their roots made as much for the New York they occasionally inhabit as from inner necessity. Whereas in the past a mythology was given to the artist by tradition and patron, in the post-modern world it is chosen and constructed.

In the mid-seventies, Mariani created his fictional academy of eighteenth-century peers – Goethe, Winckelmann, Mengs, etc – and then painted some missing canvasses to fill out a mythic history. In the early 1980s he transferred this mythology to the present day and painted an allegory of a post-modern Parnassus, with friends, enemies, critics and dealers collected around himself. This is the typical post-modern trope – an ironic comment on a comment on a comment which signals the distance; a new myth thrice removed from its originating ritual. The painting is a contemporary rendition of Raphael's and Meng's versions of the traditional subject. The texts are layered on top of one another as enigmatic commentary; like the structure of traditional myth, there is reiteration, but unlike this structure there is self-conscious irony. Perhaps too much?

The work is a fine line between pastiche and parody. The facial expressions and detail suggest both intentions. Mariani, solemn and supercilious, sits below Ganymede being abducted to heaven by Zeus. Ganymede is not only the beautiful boy of Greek mythology being captured in the erotic embrace of the eagle Zeus, but a portrait of the performance artist Luigi Ontani; hence the hoop and stick. To the right, Francesco Clemente gazes past a canvas held by Sandro Chia; Mario Merz is Hercules in an understated bathtub; a well-known New York art dealer waddles to the water personified as a turtle; critics write and admire their own profiles. All this is carried out in the mock-heroic style of the late eighteenth century,

[25] Carlo Maria Mariani, **Costellazioni del Leone (La Scuola di Roma)**, 1980-1, oil on canvas, 340 x 452cm. An elaborate allegory on the current Post-Modern School of Rome – one part eighteenth-century pastiche, one part critical satire. (Courtesy of Sperone Westwater Gallery, New York)

[26] Eric Fischl, **A Brief History of North Africa**, 1985, oil on linen, 223.5 x 305cm. Fischl explores archetypal scenes – the beach, the suburban backyard, the bedroom – for their latent violence and sexuality. The atmosphere is often charged with a dissociated passion that reveals the vulnerability of character and the ambiguity of political and social roles. (Courtesy of Mary Boone Gallery, New York)

[27] Ron Kitaj, **If Not, Not**, 1975-6, oil on canvas, 152.4 x 152.4cm. This most serious post-modern painter often used modernist themes and characters as a departure point for his fractured allegories. These sustain a mood of catastrophe and mystery which is alleviated by small emblems of hope and a haunting beauty. (Courtesy of Scottish National Gallery of Modern Art, Edinburgh)

the style of *La Pittura Colta* which Mariani has made his own. No one who gives this 'cultured painting' a second look would confuse it for the real thing, or as straight revivalist, although many critics unsympathetic to Post-Modernism have branded the work as 'fascist'. The representational conventions had been dismissed by Modernists as taboo, as frigid academic art (admittedly, Mariani leaves his renditions at the level of stereotype).

If Mariani constructs his own mythology, then so do many Post-Modernists who are involved in allegory and narrative. This concern for content is comparable to architects' renewed concern for symbolism and meaning. Whereas Modernism, and particularly Late-Modernism, concentrated on the autonomy and expression of the individual art form – the aesthetic dimension – Post-Modernists focus on the semantic aspect. This generalisation is true of such different artists as David Hockney, Malcolm Morley, Eric Fischl, Lennart Anderson and Paul Georges, some [2 of whom have painted enigmatic allegories and others a combination of sexual and classical narratives. The so-called 'return to painting' of the 1980s is also a return to a traditional concern with content, although it is content with a difference from pre-modern art.

Again, because these Post-Modernists have had a modern training, they are inevitably concerned with abstraction and the basic reality of modern life; that is, a secular mass-culture dominated by economic and pragmatic motives. When they treat religious and cultural subject matter, they reveal its socially constructed nature. This gives their work the same complexity, mannerism and double coding present in post-modern architecture, and also an eclectic or hybrid style.

One of the most accomplished post-modern artists, Ron Kitaj, goes [beyond the easy irony of those such as Mariani, to deal with the essential problem of modern life after Modernism. Kitaj, the Jewish-American émigré who lives in London, is the artist most concerned with cultural subject matter – something for which London critics will not forgive him. His 1994 retrospective at the Tate Gallery was savaged by modern reviewers such as Andrew Graham Dixon because he committed the ultimate sin of making literary and autobiographical content explicit. Characteristically, he confronts modernist techniques of collage and flat, graphic composition with Renaissance traditions, just as he places the Holocaust – and its modernist causes – in opposition to a more healthy situation, whether a natural landscape or cityscape. His enigmatic allegory *If Not, Not* is a visual counterpart of TS Eliot's *The Wasteland*, on which it is partly based. Survivors of war crawl through the desert towards an oasis; survivors of civilisation (including Eliot himself) are engaged in quizzical acts, some with representatives of exotic culture. Lamb, crow, palm tree, turquoise lake and a Tuscan landscape consciously adapted from the classical tradition resonate with common overtones. They point towards a Western and Christian background overlaid by Modernism, the cult of primitivism and disaster. The classical barn/monument at the top, so reminiscent of Aldo Rossi and post-modern face buildings, also suggests the death camps (it actually represents Auschwitz). Indeed the burning inferno of the sky, the corpse and broken pier, the black and truncated trees all suggest life after the Second World War, after the last slaughter by the mechanised culture that is modernity. It is a view of life as plural, confused and tortured on the whole, but containing islands of peace (and a search for wholeness). The title, with its double negative – *If Not, Not* – was taken from an ancient political oath which meant roughly, if you the King do not uphold our liberties and laws, then we do not uphold you. Thus, the consequences of broken promises and fragmented culture are the content of this gripping drama, one given a classical *gravitas* set against modernist rupture. The extreme oppositions are artistic equivalents of Stirling's Stuttgart.

Examples of this type of narrative, with its suggestive moral allegory, could be multiplied. Robert Rauschenberg, David Salle, Hans Haacke, Ian Hamilton-Finlay and Eric Fischl invoke the classical tradition while portraying contemporary culture. Their specific ethical views differ widely, but their general intention to transform the classical tradition of a political and moral art is shared. In this sense there is some commonality to all the Post-Modernists mentioned, an agenda which loosely unites architects, artists and writers such as Umberto Eco, David Lodge, John Barth, Salmon Rushdie and those discussed in Linda Hutcheon's *A Poetics of Postmodernism*.[39] There is the intention to confront the present with the past, to question and subvert from within the dominating culture, to represent the complexity of contemporary life through double coding. However, not all those who left High Modernism jumped over the 'post', and that has led to some deep misunderstandings to which we now turn.

THE CONFUSION OF LATE- WITH POST-MODERNISM

Every movement in history has contradictory forces and contending groups, and these contradictions can be fruitful, often leading to new developments, as in science, when one paradigm develops from the inconsistencies of the previous one. Modernism, as I have mentioned, is progressivist in architecture and reactionary in other disciplines, and there are further oppositions within the broad movement. Although creative, such contradictions cause confusion. To deal with this I shall resort, as Frank Kermode and Robert

[28] Ian Hamilton-Finlay, **Nuclear Sail**, 1974, slate (with John Andrew). The ambiguous beauty of war machines is often a departure point for Finlay's combination of emblem, writing and sculpture. Here the black 'sail' of a Polaris submarine stands against an artificial lake with the title engraved beside it: the ambiguity of the sail/conning tower is thus extended to that of a dolmen and black tombstone. Terror and virtue, destruction and beauty are two sides to Finlay's art as in military iconography. (C Jencks)

39 Linda Hutcheon, *A Poetics of Postmodernism, History, Theory, Fiction*, Routledge (New York/London), 1988, pp3-22.

*[29] Renzo Piano and Richard Rogers, **Pompidou Centre**, Paris 1971-7. The modernist emphasis on structure, circulation, open space, industrial detailing and abstraction is taken to its late-modern extreme, although again often mis-termed post-modern. (C Jencks)*

Stern have done, to technical terms, because the word 'modern' hides at least two different meanings.[40]

There is the healing role of the artist, that of overcoming the 'split between thinking and feeling' (which TS Eliot and Siegfried Giedion located in the nineteenth century), and this leads to what has been called 'Heroic Modernism'. Then there is the subversive role of the artist; conquering new territory, to make art destructive, difficult, and dramatically suffering – what I, following Renato Poggioli, would call 'Agonistic' Modernism.

Agonism means tension: the pathos of a Laocoon struggling in his ultimate spasm to make his own suffering immortal and fecund. In short, agonism means sacrifice and consecration – an hyperbolic passion, a bow bent towards the impossible, a paradoxical and positive form of spiritual defeatism.[41]

Heroic versus Agonistic Modernism relates to what Stern labels 'traditional versus schismatic Modernism'; that is, humanism versus anti-humanism, continuity versus 'the shock of the new', tragic optimism versus nihilism, creative versus destructive transcendence and so on. For Stern, and writers such as Ihab Hassan, Schismatic Modernism has itself mutated into Schismatic Post-Modernism. Thus Hassan asserts that 'Postmodernism is essentially subversive in form and anarchic in its cultural spirit. It dramatises its lack of faith in art even as it produces new works of art intended to hasten both cultural and artistic dissolution.'[42]

Artistic dissolution – a strange, but typically agonistic goal. As examples Hassan mentions the literature of Genet and Beckett, what George Steiner calls the 'literature of silence'; the self-abolishing art of Tinguely and Robert Morris, the mechanistic and repetitive art of Warhol, the non-structural music of John Cage and the technical architecture of Buckminster Fuller.[43] Much of this Post-War work (except Fuller) takes Early Modernism, and Futurist notions of radical discontinuity, to the extreme, and this leads directly to the hermeticism of the 1960s and 1970s.

Thus arises the central confusion. Because this later tradition was obviously different from the Heroic Modernism of the 1920s, quite a few critics loosely applied the prefix 'post'. For instance, in referring to architecture, the journalists Paul Goldberger and Douglas Davis used it in the *New York Times* and *Newsweek* to discuss the ultra-modern work of Hardy, Holzman and Pfeiffer, Cesar Pelli, and Kevin Roche, all of which exaggerates the High-Tech architecture of Mies and Le Corbusier.[44] The art critic Edward Lucie-Smith, as did others, even applied it to Piano and Rogers' Pompidou Centre in Paris.[45] In short, this Postmodernism meant everything that was different from High-Modernism, and usually this meant

40 The two basic strands of Modernism are discussed by many critics. *See* for instance Renato Poggioli, *The Theory of The Avant-Garde*, Harvard University Press (Cambridge, Mass.), 1968. The discussion of Bradbury and McFarlane is particularly relevant; *see* their 'The Name and Nature of Modernism', in *Modernism 1890-1930* edited by Malcolm Bradbury and James McFarlane, Penguin Books (Harmondsworth), 1976, pp40-41, 46; Frank Kermode, 'Modernisms', in *Modern Essays* (London), 1971. For architecture the best discussion is Robert Stern, 'The Doubles of Post-Modern', *The Harvard Architectural Review*, Vol 1, Spring 1980, although, as my text makes clear, I would use the term Late-Modern for his 'Schismatic Post-Modern'.

41 Renato Poggioli, *The Theory of the Avant-Garde*, Harvard University Press (Cambridge Mass), 1968, p66.

42 Ihab Hassan, 'Joyce, Beckett, and the postmodern imagination', *Tri Quarterly* XXXIV Fall 1975, p200.

43 Ihab Hassan, Paracriticisms: *Seven Speculations of the Times*, University of Illinois Press (Urbana), 1975, pp55-6.

44 For references *see The Language of Post-Modern Architecture*, Fourth edition (Academy Editions), London, 1984, p8.

45 The work of Archigram and Richard Rogers was often termed Post-Modern in the late 1970s before critics began to understand the term and its distinction from High-Tech. Edward Lucie-Smith followed this usage in his book on Modernism published in *Reallife*, 30 March 1981.

skyscrapers with funny shapes, brash colours and exposed technology. That such architects were against the pluralism, convention and thirty or so definers of the post-modern agenda was missed by these critics, and their many followers. They just adopted a current phrase for the shift from Modernism and lumped most departures under it.

The same permissive categorisation was practised in artistic theory and criticism. Consequently, when conferences were held on the subject, artists were confused as to whether they were supporting the post-modern or were against it.[46] Indeed an influential anthology, *The Anti-Aesthetic: Essays on Postmodern Culture*, was dedicated to this confusion.[47] Here, the editor Hal Foster, uses it to mean a cultural and political resistance to the status quo. For another contributor, Craig Owens, it means the critical use of post-industrial techniques (computers and photography) in art, and the 'loss of master narratives' (in this, he follows Jean-François Lyotard). Frederic Jameson uses it as an umbrella term to cover all reactions to High-Modernism (again John Cage and William Burroughs); the levelling of distinctions between high and mass-culture and two of its 'significant features' – pastiche and schizophrenia. Jean Baudrillard refers to it in a totalistic way as epitomising our era and its 'death of the subject', caused by television and the information revolution. ('We live in the ecstasy of communication. And this ecstasy is obscene.')[48] Most of the remaining authors use it in further ways, some of which have a relation to resisting or 'deconstructing' the common assumptions of our culture. In short, most of the uses follow agonistic traditions of the new.

Rosalind Krauss' essay 'Sculpture in the Expanded Field', printed in another anthology, shows the usage.[49] Her witty essay seeks to define all departures from sculpture that appear to break down the category of modernist sculpture – for example, Brancusi's *Endless Column* – and expand them to include such things as Christo's *Running Fence* and wrapped buildings, Robert Smithson's use of earth-covered mirrors in the Yucatan, a wooden maze by Alice Aycock constructed in 1972, and various earth-works, and 'marked sites', such as a sunken, framed hole in the ground executed by Mary Miss in 1978.

Krauss uses a structuralist diagram to draw this expanded field of sculpture – the objects that are not architecture, not landscape, indeed not sculpture – and her wit consists in making the diagram itself expand to include a lot of combined 'nots'. The strategy is not dissimilar to the modernist practice of defining things by what they are not, in order to maximise their differences, but she presents their expansion as a 'rupture' with Modernism:

One after another Robert Morris, Robert Smithson, Michael Heizer,

[30] Robert Morris, **Untitled 1970**, *brown felt, 182.9 x 548.6cm, installed 243.8cm high. Sculpture, as Rosalind Krauss defines it, becoming 'pure negativity: the combination of exclusions . . . a kind of ontological absence'. Morris, in the late 1960s, reached some interestingly elegant dead ends such as here with the dark felt which, with its subtle logical twists, tells you it is 'not wall and not floor' but what is left over when you subtract these. (Courtesy of Saatchi Collection, London)*

46 'Post-Modernism', a symposium at the Institute for Architecture and Urban Studies, 1981, attended by Christian Hubert, Sherrie Levine, Craig Owens, David Salle and Julian Schnabel, later published in *Reallife*, 30 March 1981.

47 *The Anti-Aesthetic: Essays on Postmodern Culture*, edited by Hal Foster, Bay Press (Port Townsend), Washington 1983.

48 Ibid, p130.

49 Ibid, pp31-42. *See also* the anthology *Theories of Contemporary Art* edited by Richard Hertz, Prentice Hall (New Jersey), 1985, pp215-25. Post-Modernism is also discussed by various authors in a loose way in this anthology.

[31] Sol LeWitt, **Serial Project (A, B, C, D)**, 1966, white stove enamel on aluminium, 92.9 x 574.5 x 575cm. A series of mechanical operations carried out by others lend these geometrical works an architectural flavour. Ultimately this automatic sculpture, like the architectural machines of Hiromi Fujii and Peter Eisenman, is very beautiful in the way its white grids pop up everywhere like rabbits. Why the series isn't titled A, B, C, D, E, F, as mathematically would seem to be implied, is a proposition to contemplate. Conceptual and Minimalist art were both typical late-modern movements. (Courtesy of Saatchi Collection, London)

Richard Serra, Walter de Maria, Robert Irwin, Sol LeWitt, Bruce Nauman (between 1968 and 1970) had entered a situation the logical conditions of which can no longer be described as modernist.[50]

In her diagrammatic terms, this is quite true. However, she then goes on to make a false inference:

In order to name this historical rupture and the structural transformation of the cultural field that characterizes it, one must have recourse to another term. The one already in use in other areas of criticism is postmodernism. There seems no reason not to use it.[51]

Oh yes there is not – to use the not-way of not-definition – for, if one thing is not obscure, it is that you cannot define things usefully by what they are not. All the things in a room that are not men are not necessarily women; there is a near infinity of other classes of things. And those artists she mentions are not Post-Modernists, but really Late-Modernists. Why? Because, like ultra or Neo-Modernists, they take modernist disjunction and abstraction to an extreme. Essentially their practice goes against the thirty or so definers of Post-Modernism I have mentioned – all those connected with respect for existing cultures. Their work is much closer to Agonistic Modernism, except it is more extreme, exaggerated; in short, 'Late'.

This leads to the essential definition of Late-Modernism. In architecture it is pragmatic and technocratic in its social ideology and, from about 1960, takes many of the stylistic ideas and values of Modernism to an extreme in order to resuscitate a dull (or clichéd) language.[52] Late-modern art is also coded singly in this way and, like the Modernism of Clement Greenberg, tends to be self-referential and involved with its art-specific language, even minimalist in this concentration, as so many critics such as Umberto Eco have pointed out.[53]

What I am suggesting is not a minor shift in nomenclature, but a complete reshuffling of categories; to redefine as mostly 'Late' what Davis, Goldberger, Foster, Jameson, Lyotard, Baudrillard, Krauss, Hassan and so many others often define as 'Post'. It is mostly 'Late' because it is still committed to the tradition of the new and does not have a complex relation to the past, or pluralism, or the transformation of Western culture, or a concern with meaning, continuity and symbolism. I doubt these writers will agree with me, but I do believe that what is at stake is more than a pedantic distinction. It is a difference of values and philosophy. To call a Late-Modernist a Post-Modernist is tantamount to calling a Protestant a Catholic because they both practise a Christian religion, or to criticise a donkey for being a bad sort of horse. Such category mistakes invariably lead to misreadings, which may in themselves may be very fruitful and creative (the Russians read

50 *The Anti-Aesthetic: Essays on Postmodern Culture*, edited by Hal Foster, Bay Press, Port Townsend (Washington), 1983, p39.

51 Ibid.

52 I proposed this essential definition of Late-Modernism, along with those of Modernism and Post-Modernism, in *AD News* 7/81 and they were later published in *Transactions 3*, RIBA, London, 1983, pp37-40.

53 See notes 13 (p19), 32 (p31), and 34 (p32) for some of those who also distinguish Late- from Post-Modernism in related ways.

Don Quixote as a tragedy) but it is ultimately a violation of the work.

Try to read Norman Foster's Hongkong and Shanghai Bank as a post-modern building and you will get as far as the 'non-door', where the two escalators are shifted at an angle to accommodate the Chinese principle of Feng Shui. Is it contextual, related to the buildings surrounding it and the vernaculars of Hong Kong and China? Only in the most oblique sense that it is 'high-tech', and one side has a thin, picturesque group of towers. Is it involved with the 'taste-cultures' of the users? Only in the subliminal sense that its 'skin and bones' suggest muscle power. According to the agonistic reading of Postmodernism it should be a member of this class, because it is a 'rupture' with Modernism and fully committed to the tradition of the new. Indeed most of its parts, adopted from aeroplane and ship technology, were purpose-built in different parts of the globe precisely to be new. It is the first radically 'multinational' building – parts were fabricated in Britain, Japan, Austria, Italy and America – resolved by all the technologies of the post-industrial society, including of course, the computer. In addition it was created by instant world communication. Because of all this, according to the definitions of Jean-François Lyotard and Frederic Jameson, it should be a prime example of Post-Modernism. But it is not and, if it were, it would be a failure.

In fact, it has to be judged as a triumph of Late-Modernism and celebrated for what Foster (who hates Post-Modernism) intends it to be; namely, the most powerful expression of structural trusses, lightweight technology, and huge open space stacked internally in the air. The cost of the building – it is called the most expensive building in the world – directly reflects these intentions, for it turns out that the money went on the bridge-like structure and the superb use of finishing materials, which are surprising areas to take up so much of a budget. Thus, I do not mean to criticise the building for its post-modern shortcomings, but to support it for its late-modern virtues. These are, as usual, the imaginative and consistent use of the technical language of architecture. The morality of Late-Modernism consists in this integrity of invention and usage; like Clement Greenberg's defence of modernist morality the work has to be judged as a hermetic, internally related world, where the meanings are self-referential. Literally, does the High-Tech fit together and work, visually, poetically and functionally? The answers appear to be positive.

The concept of Post-Modernism is often confused with Late-Modernism because they both spring from a post-industrial society. Indeed there is a connection between these two 'posts', but not the direct one that the philosopher Jean-François Lyotard implies. He opens his book *The*

[32] Norman Foster, **Hongkong and Shanghai Bank**, 1982-6. *Post-modern failure, late-modern triumph. The structure is totally designed all the way through, fairly flexible and extremely expensive. A corporate Rolls Royce it epitomises the contradictions of modernity: egalitarian and hierarchical. (C Jencks)*

Postmodern Condition: A Report on Knowledge with the elision of the two terms:

> The object of this study is the condition of knowledge in the most highly developed societies. I have decided to use the word postmodern to describe that condition . . . I define postmodern as incredulity towards metanarratives . . . Our working hypothesis is that the status of knowledge is altered as societies enter what is known as the post-industrial age and cultures enter what is known as the postmodern age.[54]

Lyotard's study is mostly concerned with knowledge in our scientific age; in particular the way it is legitimised through the 'grand narratives' such as the liberation of humanity, progress, the emancipation of the proletariat, and increased economic power. These 'master narratives', he contends, have gone the way of previous ones such as religion, the nation-state and the belief in the destiny of the West. They have become non-credible, incredible. Indeed, all beliefs or master narratives become impossible in a scientific age, including the ultimate legitimacy of science itself. Hence the nihilism and anarchism he speaks of in 'language games' which fight each other, but also his pluralism and belief that postmodern culture entails a 'sensitivity to differences' and a 'war on totality'.[55]

The postmodern is then defined as 'a period of slackening', a period in which everything is 'delegitimised'. Given this nihilism and propensity for extreme formulations, one can understand why the Sunday reporter at *Le Monde* [56] was so upset by the spectre about to descend like a fog onto the breakfast table. Lyotard has almost defined Postmodernism as this 'slackening'. But in another section, amazingly, he defines it as pre-modern:

> What space does Cézanne challenge? The Impressionists'. What object do Picasso and Braque attack? Cézanne's . . . A work can become modern only if it is first postmodern. Postmodernism thus understood is not modernism at its end but in the nascent state, and this state is constant.[57]

This crazy idea has at least the virtue of being original, and it has led to Lyotard's belief in continual experiment, the agonism of the perpetual avant-garde and continual revolution. The expression of this idea may be paradoxical and hard to follow, but it is interesting and worth analysing. Ultimately it leads to his notion of the sublime, the ultimate difference 'of which one cannot speak' (shades of Wittgenstein):

> The postmodern would be that which, in the modern, puts forward the unpresentable in presentation itself . . . The rules and categories [of the postmodern work are not pre-established but] are what the work of art is looking for . . . Post modern would have to be understood according to the paradox of the future (post) anterior (modo).[58]

In effect it is the rules of the game, the philosophical status of art, which

54 Jean-François Lyotard, *The Postmodern Condition: A Report on Knowledge*, Manchester University Press, 1984, ppXXIII, XIV, 3. The book was first published in French in 1979.

55 Ibid, ppXXV and 82.

56 Gerard-Georges Lemaire, 'Le Spectre du post-modernisme', 'Decadence', *Le Monde Dimanche*, 18 October 1981, pXIV.

57 Jean-François Lyotard, *The Postmodern Condition: A Report on Knowledge*. Manchester University Press, 1984, p79.

58 Ibid, p81.

the postmodern artist challenges in order to recreate. It is as if every good artist had to be an Einstein overthrowing a previous Newtonian paradigm. This fanatical pursuit of overturning assumptions rules out the post-modern commitment to micro-creativity, invention within a language, as well as its obligation to the local community. Lyotard hates the idea of consensus, any social totality, and his alliance with the artists of the sublime makes him the extreme individualist – that is, an Ultra-Modernist.

To reiterate, Lyotard is confusing Late with Post-Modernism. Thus we are at a 'crisis' point – to use one of his concepts of legitimisation – over whether to go on using the word post-modern to encompass two opposite meanings and diverging traditions. It is literally nonsense to continue with this linguistic confusion. Furthermore, I would argue that the meanings and definitions I have proposed – dichotomising late and post-modern – gain in power precisely to the extent that they are used together, because these traditions oppose each other dialectically.

Having stated the case for a distinction between Post and Late-Modernism, I should, however, add some refinements which do not make it absolute. Both traditions start around 1960, both react to the wane of Modernism and some artists and architects – for instance David Salle, Robert Longo, Mario Botta, Michael Hopkins and Arata Isozaki – either vacillate between or unite the two. This overlap, or existential mixing of categories, is found in other periods. After the Renaissance, for instance, an artist such as Michelangelo moved from Early to High Renaissance, Mannerist and Baroque solutions to resolve sculptural and architectural problems.

I agree, therefore, that there are many artists whom Hal Foster *et al* include in their corpus as 'postmodernists of resistance' who should also be included as Post-Modernists – Robert Rauschenberg, Laurie Anderson, some feminist art which uses conventional subject matter in an ironic way, Hans Haacke and others who are occasionally agonistic and combative. But, I would insist, they should be so classified only in so far as their intention was to communicate with society and its professional elites through the use of double coding. More importantly, even if such artists are termed post-modern, it does not guarantee their value which must depend, as before, on their creativity and depth, and the imaginative transformation of a shared symbolic system. These are trans-cultural values.

[33] Michael Hopkins, **Bracken House**, London, Albert Richardson, 1959, redesigned by Hopkins, 1991. Hopkins has been labelled 'the acceptable face of Modernism', in a slightly damning way, because Prince Charles found his Lords Cricket Ground decorous. It makes as much sense to call him the 'Mies of Post-Modernism' because his reductivist structuralism always carries references to context, history and different tastes. In any case, there are several artists and architects who fall clearly between categories, and Hopkins is one of integrity. (C Jencks)

PART THREE

POST-MODERN SOCIETY

THE POST-MODERN INFORMATION WORLD
AND THE RISE OF THE COGNITARIAT

In the late nineteenth century, the French poet Comte de Lautréamont defined beauty as 'the fortuitous encounter of a sewing machine and an umbrella on a dissection table'. Bizarre, convulsive juxtaposition – sometimes beautiful and very unusual. In the late twentieth century a traditionally-garbed Bedouin can be found riding a camel across the desert while having, beneath his robes, a business suit, mobile phone and laptop computer. I have been on the tenth floor of a High-Tech tower in Tokyo and watched seven traditional Japanese weddings going on at once. Today incongruity is usual.

The most visible shift in the post-modern world is towards pluralism and cultural eclecticism; an heterogeneity which was never intentional. Pluralism is mostly a by-product of communication and global capitalism, and many nations would wish it away. But the globe has been irreversibly united by current technologies into an instantaneous, twenty-four-hour information world, the post-industrial successor to a modern world based on relatively, by today's standards, snail-paced industry.

Some nations are dissolving, and all national identities are hybridising. Cultural boundaries are now crossed easily because of increasing trade, ease of travel and immediate world communication. This has led to 'space-time compression', the 'global village', which miniaturises the earth spatially and temporally to the equivalent of a small town – perhaps even a computer console.[59] The space and time necessary for a transaction, meeting or media event has imploded drastically while the speed with which capitalism forces styles to change and products to innovate has also modified our taste for change in schizophrenic ways. Media cultures are at once more stereotyping – and in that sense conservative – and hooked on constant marginal variation.

Such combustible changes have created 'the post-modern condition', bringing unique opportunities and problems. This duality is why the condition cannot be entirely supported or condemned; the only intelligent attitude is critical selection, to choose or 'eclect' the positive elements and try to suppress the negative (not that this is always possible). For instance, the much proclaimed 'end of work', which the post-industrial society is bringing, shows a Janus face; there is both more leisure time and job insecurity, work variety and exploitation. But no country has yet been able to have the former goals without the latter by-products.

[34] **Japanese wedding on the tenth floor**. *A twenty-storey steel skyscraper by Nikken Sekki, 1973, holds as many incongruous functions as the front page of a newspaper. (C Jencks)*

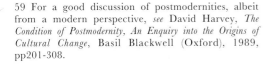

59 For a good discussion of postmodernities, albeit from a modern perspective, *see* David Harvey, *The Condition of Postmodernity, An Enquiry into the Origins of Cultural Change*, Basil Blackwell (Oxford), 1989, pp201-308.

To understand the post-modern condition is to grasp such contrasts. This mental act is hard because there is no one principle. How does one decode a kaleidoscope, or comprehend city traffic? Not by focusing down, but by panning up to see the general pattern. The post-modern condition shows a series of simultaneous slides from one situation to another; none of them are complete, all of them are hybrid.

There is the partial shift from mass-production to segmented production (from Fordism to Post-Fordism); the slide from a relatively integrated mass-culture to many fragmented taste cultures (minoritisation); from centralised control in government and business to peripheral decision-making; from repetitive manufacture of identical objects to the fast-changing manufacture of varying objects; from few styles to many genres; from national identification to both local and global consciousness.

There are many more related changes than this short list implies, but one of the deep causes of change is what Daniel Bell fully analysed in 1973 as the Post-Industrial Society (sixty years after it had been predicted); others call it the 'Third Wave', or 'information society'.[60] Several related events brought it into existence.

Contemplate this kaleidoscope of change. In 1956, in the USA, for the first time the number of white collar workers outnumbered blue collar workers, and by the late 1970s America had made the shift to an information society, with relatively few people – 13 per cent – involved in the manufacture of goods. Most workers – 60 per cent – were engaged in the manufacture of signs and symbols, information and knowledge. Whereas a modernised society depended on most people mass-producing objects in a factory (30 per cent), the post-modernised one depends on the segmented production of ideas and images in an office (by about the same percentage). Very few of the population today are farmers – in the modern world of 1900 they constituted 30 per cent of the labour force; in the post-modern world they make up from 3 to 10 per cent (USA and Japan). The service sector has fluctuated over the last ten years at around 11 to 12 per cent of the workforce, about the same percentage as unemployment.

In the post-modern world, a fundamental social fact is the revolutionary growth of those who create and pass on information. Put another way, it [35] is the sudden emergence of a new class; the numerical domination of the proletariat by the cognitariat. These new workers are neither working class nor really middle class, but rather paraclass. They cut across customary boundaries and make for volatile political allegiances. Who can predict how the electorate will feel next week? Statistically, most of the paraclass are clerks, secretaries, insurance people, stockbrokers, teachers, managers,

60 Daniel Bell, 'Notes on the Post-Industrial Society' I&II, *The Public Interest*, Spring, 1967; *The Coming of the Post-Industrial Society*, 1973; Alvin Toffler, *The Third Wave*, William Collins and Sons (London), 1980.

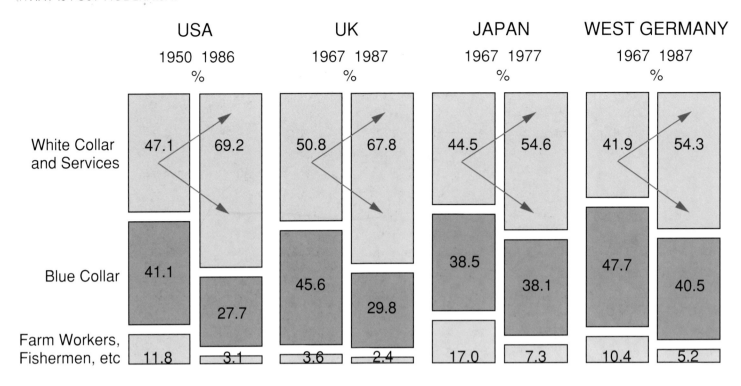

	USA		UK		JAPAN		WEST GERMANY	
	1950	1986	1967	1987	1967	1977	1967	1987
	%		%		%		%	
White Collar and Services	47.1	69.2	50.8	67.8	44.5	54.6	41.9	54.3
Blue Collar	41.1	27.7	45.6	29.8	38.5	38.1	47.7	40.5
Farm Workers, Fishermen, etc	11.8	3.1	3.6	2.4	17.0	7.3	10.4	5.2

[35] **Sectoral slides**. *The growth of the white collar is accompanied by the decline of the blue collar and farming sectors.*

governmental bureaucrats, lawyers, writers, bankers, technicians, programmers, accountants and ad-men. Indeed, in the First World there is a plague of public relations agents and those manipulating the 'consciousness industry'. Why has this happened? Because prime time television and prime space in the quality media are both in very short supply (given the near infinite demand). You can mine gold in many countries, but there is only one *New York Times*, BBC, and *Le Monde*. In the post-modern world the fierce competition is for media validation and this multiplies another part of the cognitariat – the chattering classes, the opinion-formers and the opinionated.

Salaries of the cognitariat differ as much as their way of life and status and are finely graded, from cognicrats at the top to cogniproles at the bottom. The fundamental fact of the post-industrial society is that, as Daniel Bell made clear in the 1970s, knowledge, not ownership, is power. To navigate through the burgeoning information world takes social skills, a certain intelligence and applied knowledge. This is why, in spite of all the new labour-saving devices, the work done by the cognicrats at the top has not diminished. As John Kenneth Galbraith has shown, with his concept of the 'technostructure', it now takes a small army of experts to launch any advanced industrial product such as a new car; teams of accountants, lawyers, advertisers, not to say designers, technicians and inventors. If there is any final control in this situation it is not just ownership, but the ability to manipulate knowledge. This is where the ultimate power rests – with the cognicrats and their teams of market analysts and experts.

Class-analysis of the old type does not work in this new situation; the proletariat versus the capitalist. The cognitariat paraclass is too big and amorphous to find the old, sharp divisions. Perhaps a new polarisation is emerging, as Will Hutton argues of Britain: 'the 30/30/40 society'.[61] The bottom 30 per cent are the unemployed or economically inactive, the top 40 per cent are the full-time employed and self-employed, and the middle 30 per cent are the part-timers and casual workers – the relatively insecure. While these structural facts exist throughout the post-modern world, they do not relate closely to individual identity as, for instance, did working class culture. Furthermore, there is some mobility within the cognitariat and certainly lots of job changing. Thus, social distinctions dissolve and cultural identifiers – accent, dress, social attitudes and values – become fuzzy. Lastly, the new productive mode called flexible specialisation, 'flexitime', leads to a constant rotation of jobs. This is a defining aspect of the emergent Post-Fordism.

Post-Fordism is just as essential to the post-modern condition as post-industrialisation. It gathers momentum after the oil shock of 1973 and the economic stagnation of large Fordist enterprises that had been the cornerstone of modernity ever since Henry Ford defined the modern corporation in the 1920s. By the early 1980s the strongest growth was Post-Fordist; that is, in small, fast-changing companies of less than fifty people who are networked by computer and other media. Flexible specialisation, just-in-time production, allowing small stockpiles and a quick response to changing fashions, characterise the system. A company such as Benetton manages many such dispersed networks and engages in little if any actual production.

Post-Fordist and Fordist enterprises are necessarily tightly interwoven. All advanced economies are radically hybrid, and no single sector leads them. In the typical case they are interrelated wholes, with one-third of the economy being Fordist, one-third Post-Fordist and the remaining third state supported. Such purified types as 'socialism' or 'capitalism' do not capture this mixture. Perhaps the compound 'socitalism' – socialised capitalism – gets closer to the truth; that advanced economies depend on dynamic mixtures between the large, the small, the state and the hybrid whole. As the Post-Communist world shows, it is much easier to socialise capitalism than capitalise socialism. The economies which are most resilient recognise the marketplace, but do not fetishise competition and privatisation. That is why the 'social market' became the catchphrase by the late eighties,

61 Will Hutton, *The State We're In*, Jonathan Cape (London), 1995.

[36] **Shoko Asahara as media event**. *Japanese television was dominated by the cult leader for several months thus, ironically, framing a negative event with positive attention; the same inversion was characteristic of the Prince Charles Affair in Britain and the OJ Simpson Trial in the USA. Nothing sells like bad news except conspiritorial bad news.*

and many European countries tried to get the exact mixture of socialism right. The problem is that this balance changes dynamically in the global market.

So much for basic abstractions. It may sound rather benevolent; in the First World it has meant the end of the working class and the decline of class antagonisms. The 60 to 80 per cent of the population in the paraclass is, in some material ways, better off than was its modern predecessor. But the obvious downside is present in virtually all post-modern societies; a widening gap between rich and poor, those who command an information-society and those who are left behind; the loss of working class culture and the despair of those now trapped in a new underclass.

Another negative consequence of these fast-moving trends is the confusion of identities and beliefs so that cults and sects and trivial private affairs dominate the news. Is it a surprise that the private lives of Prince Charles and Princess Diana monopolised the British media for three years? Or that the OJ Simpson Trial and 'the Sarin Gas Sect' (as it is quaintly known) were top of the consciousness industry in America and Japan for a year? Reformed actors such as Ronald Reagan dominate vast numbers of the population – in spite of the fact that few may believe in these media-masks very deeply. After Reagan vacated the presidency, his followers dropped him with a shrug when he took up advertising in Japan. Easy belief equals easy disillusion; not even anger sticks to the Teflon President.

The way once effective media-bytes are soon forgotten can be brought out by a series of questions. Can you remember who called Reagan's deficit spending 'voodoo economics'? George Bush, the man who would continue the voodoo. And who beat him with the one-liner, 'It's the economy, stupid'? Yes, Clinton, the president whose popularity went *down* when the economy went *up*. Moral? Politicians cannot remember their own slogans, which have little bearing on the truth, anyway. It is no surprise they are believed in only weakly. Weak thought, weak belief and social insecurities are some of the endemic problems of the post-modern condition.

THE POST-NATIONAL WORLD: CULTURE ACCELERATION

As important as the information society and Post-Fordism is the organised network of world communication which allows it to function. This started at the end of the 1950s with the launch of *Sputnik*. The *Columbia* Space Shuttle of 1981 brackets the period of history when satellite communication was combined with ubiquitous jet travel, computer processing, the old-fashioned telephone and countless world circulation magazines and newspapers, to form an efficient network, a community of world producers and consumers. Since then fax, Internet, E-mail and expert systems have only streamlined the world linkage. The significant point is not the invention of this or that technology, but the sudden emergence of an integrated system of global communication.

Because of this and electronic trading, the world suddenly lost five trillion dollars on Black Monday, 19 October 1987. New York started with a big plummet, then Tokyo picked up the news. Then, as each market woke up in turn – Hong Kong, Singapore, Frankfurt, Paris and London – they adopted the same steep profile. The previous modern depression took ten years; the electronic, post-modern collapse was over in less than one.

On an economic level, the global network gives multinationals greater power to move money and products as they please. On a large scale it unites mass-audiences for sporting events and royal weddings and, on a small scale, it puts scientists, artists and individuals with similar interests in touch with each other. One reason there is no longer an artistic avant-garde, in the modern sense, is that there is no identifiable front line to advance in the world village, no group or movement that cuts across all the arts, no coherent bourgeoisie to fight, no established salon to enter. Rather there are countless individuals in Tokyo, New York, Berlin, London, Milan and other world cities all communicating and competing with each other, just as they are in the banking world.

As I mentioned, Italian artists such as Sandro Chia who feature their mythical 'roots' are just as likely to work part-time in New York as they are to retreat to the Italian countryside to re-establish their ethnic identity. If the information world has had one obvious effect on culture, it is to have put all content in question. The post-modern world is the age of quotation marks, the 'so-called' this and 'Neo' that, the self-conscious fabrication, the transformation of the past and recent present, caused by the fact that almost all cultures are now within possible instant communication with each other. The negative aspects of this are clear enough in the ersatz creations which have spread everywhere (such as Holiday Inns adopting regional styles), while the positive aspects are evident in the achievements

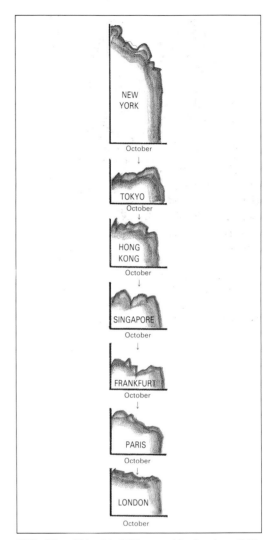

[37] **The World Village**, *19 October 1987. Instant global communication, electronic dealing systems, automated buying and selling programmes together exaggerate the market activity as the post-modern world immediately responds to the flow of information.*

[38] Sandro Chia, **Three Boys on a Raft**, 1983, oil on canvas, 246 x 282cm. Italian Futurist and mythological themes and techniques are re-used, chosen and combined for their secondary meanings. (Zindman/Fremont, Paine Weber Inc, Courtesy of Leo Castelli Gallery, New York)

of science during its multinational phase, and in the eclectic work of post-modern artists and architects.

To bring out the dramatic change that has occurred in twenty years we might adapt an anthropological system of classification; the division of historical epochs into ages, based on their fundamental forms of production (see diagram below). First is the agricultural phase of development, a result of the Neolithic Revolution, from roughly 10,000BC to 5,000BC, when 95 per cent of the population were farmers and peasants, and many of them were controlled by a priestly class ultimately governed by a king or emperor. In this pre-modern era, lasting until the birth of capitalism and the Renaissance, production was at a relatively small scale, and individuals controlled most of the property through an hierarchical society. The 'shape of time', to adopt George Kubler's phrase, was slow changing, a horizontal line punctuated fairly regularly with repetitive patterns, the cycles of work and the recurrent seasons. One could call it reversible time, since one year was very like another, unless there was war.

	production	society	space/time	orientation	culture
PRE-MODERN 10000 BC - AD1450	*Neolithic Revolution* agriculture handwork **dispersed**	*Tribal / Feudal* ruling class of kings, priests and military **peasants**	*Cyclical* slow-changing reversible time **space–time separation**	*Local / City / Empire* agrarian **closed and integrated**	*Aristocratic* integrated style **rooted cultures**
MODERN 1450 - 1960	*Industrial Revolution* factory mass-production **centralised**	*Capitalist* owning class of bourgeoisie **workers**	*Linear* sequential & progressive **space–time compression**	*Nationalist* rationalisation of business **exclusive**	*Bourgeois* reigning styles mass-culture **machine age**
POST-MODERN 1960 -	*Information Revolution* office segmented-production **decentralised**	*Socitalism* para-class of cognitariat **office workers**	*Cyclical and Linear* fast-changing **space–time implosion**	*Post-National* multinational pluralist eclectic **inclusive and open**	*Taste/ Cultures* many genres knowledge-based **age of signs**

Space and time were part of the secure background, the stage on which events occurred; space and time separated tribes and villages.

With the Renaissance and rise of capitalism in Italy and France, and then the Industrial Revolution in England and the rest of Europe, the modern world arrived. By the nineteenth century most of the population was working class, led by a bourgeoisie who commanded most of the means of production. It is a point worth stressing that the modern world tries to centralise manufacture, control it for mass-production, just as it tries to codify and regularise consumption. Mass-culture is the ultimate product of the modern world, the factory is its implicit form of organisation, and rationalisation its final value. The shape of time is now more vertical and sequential, punctuated by large-scale wars and massive population migrations. Reversible time is now countered by the linear time of history and sequential inventions. Spatial and temporal dimensions start shrinking because of inventions in communication, but nations remain relatively secure as the autonomous background on which events occur.

In the post-modern world since 1960, most of the previous relations of production alter, and the whole value system distorts. Primary products are no longer such things as automobiles, and the main industries in the First World are no longer interested in heavy equipment and steel production, but rather in information – software as well as computers, such lightweight equipment as that of air and space technology, such inventions as those in genetics and, above all, the gigantic electronics industry, the largest manufacture on the planet. In addition, this information is not 'owned', or at least monopolised, for long. Nor is it consumed by use, or decreased by reuse, as objects tend to be in the capitalist world. Quite the reverse; information multiplies itself through use, creating ever bigger circles of decision-making. Thus, unlike the previous systems of production, where an aristocracy and bourgeoisie asserted an exploitative power over a limited resource, the post-modern world is not owned, or run, or led, by any class or group, unless it is the inchoate cognitariat. This disappearance of a recognisable class with vested interests has made First World political polarisation between left and right more problematic and has given birth to new agenda politics; issues of gender, ecology and distributive justice.

The kaleidoscopic shifts from a pre-modern to post-modern world can be seen by recognising the patterns underneath my comparative diagram and, in this section and the next, I will continue to analyse these emergent formations.

In the post-modern era the shape of time rises steeply towards the vertical as world events affect each other in a chain reaction, as generations seem

[39] *Three Forms of Society. This classification is mostly based on the production process without assuming a Marxist bias that the means and relations of production entirely determine the other areas. The network of relations assumes a mutually determining system which is only likely, not inevitable. Furthermore, the post-modern is an inclusive culture which values pluralism.*

[40] Barbara Kruger, **Untitled (You are not Yourself)**, 1983, gelatin silver print, 182.9 x 122cm.

[41] Anselm Kiefer, **The High Priestess – The Land of Two Rivers**, two hundred lead books in two steel bookcases, 4.3m high, 7.9m long, 0.9m deep and weighing 30 tonnes, 1985-9. The role of books as a by-product of the mind – dead, catalogued thoughts waiting in monumental solemnity to be revived after some nuclear meltdown – is suggested by these lead tomes resembling parchment. The apocalyptic feeling is reinforced by the photographic images inside each huge book, often of ruined or decaying cities from afar. Kiefer, the minimalist Wagner of Post-Modernism, uses natural and artificial materials to give a presence to grand themes whose struggle is more often hinted at that faced.

to come and go much faster than the normal twenty years, as all cultural systems seem to approach the quick changing evanescence of fashion. In short, much more information is processed in ever smaller periods of time. Andy Warhol overexaggerated the speed and egalitarianism which the new media were bringing when he predicted, 'in the future everybody will be world-famous for fifteen minutes'. But this slogan has some truth. A generation in the art world, a new 'ism', now lasts about two years – one for discovery, the next for promotion. Movements and trends are declared 'dead stock' before they can mature. No matter how good or bad artists may be, or, how slow or fast they wish to develop, they have to acknowledge this world media-system and its fashion-go-round, if only to reject it. Indeed, a lot of post-modern art is directed against the exploitation and manipulation of information; in particular the satirical work of Hans Haacke, or the wry commentary art of Barbara Kruger, and of many artists who use photography and collage to comment on the media and its values.

The overall situation may not look promising, but there are positive aspects to it. For one thing, there are a good many artists working outside the market-nexus who are waiting to be discovered; the pluralism of Post-Modernism is very real, and contains a great deal of talent. For another, as the international art world approaches the conditions of fashion, the shape of time once again, and rather surprisingly, becomes reversible! Things change so fast that the linear times of development all run in sequence together. All fashions are in fashion, or rather still extant under the surface. Thus one can predict the cyclical transformation of old into new trends. A fashionable artist, suddenly rendered obsolete by the two-year swing of taste, can wait until a new version of the tradition comes round again in ten years' time. Artistic development is not impossible under these conditions, nor integrity; they just exist while the artist is both in and out of fashion. Kitaj, Rauschenberg and Kiefer among artists, and Isozaki, Hollein and Eisenman among architects have seen their fortunes rise and fall several times in thirty years.

Another positive aspect is the way ideas and information have become more significant with respect to material things, extractive industries and ownership. Since knowledge and information are the prime movers of a post-industrial society, the place of science and culture is revalorised as basic. The implications are, ironically, commercial and spiritual, a point to which I will return in conclusion. Beyond these points made in the diagram, there are three shifts, all of which increase the post-modern trend towards pluralism.

From Few Styles to Many Genres

The nineteenth century turned the choice of style into a matter of ideology, morality, party politics and *Zeitgeist*. Either you were for the Gothic Revival, or a hopeless pagan in favour of progressive engineering, or a reactionary. Fashion, moral arguments and the mental habits of a modernist era all conspired to force you into one camp or another, and if you were idiosyncratic enough to admit scepticism and a plurality of tastes, you did best to keep them private. Today, people are not noticably more tolerant, but they do keep changing their tastes, and at such speed that their successive dogmatisms look particularly silly. Furthermore, with the global village and the revival of so many competing 'Neo-Styles', the moral claims of each look more and more like wishful thinking. We have reached a paradoxical point with the breakdown of consensus, with the end of national styles and modernist ideology, where any style can be, and is, revived or continued. For instance there are now four basic kinds of Neo-Modernism extant: Reactionary Minimalism, all-white Corbusian abstraction, High-Tech sliding towards Organi-Tech and the still dominant Deconstructivism.

The noted art historian Heinrich Wölfflin once claimed that 'not everything is possible in any period'. As a logical truth this statement is unimpeachable, but it is of little use today with our *embarras de richesses*. We need rules, or pointers, to choose among the ten or so reigning styles, rational arguments for dealing with the variety of taste in the heteropolis. Los Angeles, the typical global heteropolis, has thirteen major minority groups, and over one hundred further ethnic divisions. Sweeping this heterogeneity behind an all-white technical abstraction is no longer an adequate response, as it was in the heyday of modernist universality. In an age when everyone is fast becoming a member of a new minority, architects and designers want to know how to represent variety with integrity. One strategy is to 'choose the right style for the job', a case of serial revivalism. A more ambitious approach is to mix the styles based on the situation as found – the existing tastes, urban conditions, and required functions – radical eclecticism. A third method is to fold in variety on the microscale, a recent departure developed from complexity theory. A fourth tactic, often that of the Los Angeles architects, is to provide heterogeneous materials and shapes in a language which is fresh and enigmatic. This method can be the most creative, avoiding stereotypes and the conflict of entrenched interests, but it can also produce grotesque mistakes.

From Purist to Kaleidoscopic Sensibility

The shift in mood that all this variety has brought is, as I mentioned at

[42] Richard Rogers Partnership, **Channel 4**, London, 1993-4. Rogers' most expressionist use of glass jumping around a circular entrance with a hommage to the Futurist power station in deep focus.

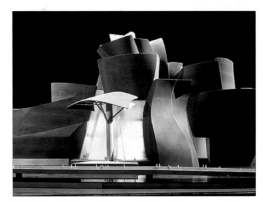

[43] Frank Gehry, **Guggenheim Museum**, Bilbao, Spain, 1992-7. A fresh and enigmatic language – twenty-six self-similar petal forms, fractals, set against rectalinear galleries – communicates difference through analogy. (F Gehry)

[44] Federico Fellini, **Ginger and Fred**. *The dark irony of an old dance couple, who did take-offs of Fred Astaire and Ginger Rogers, returning to a tv celebration to relive their past ersatz creation. The encounter of many such fabrications on a tv show creates the carnival of post-modern life, the hilarious and sad juxtapositions of disembodied tastes. (Recorded Releasing)*

the outset of this chapter, a developed taste for juxtaposition, incongruity and paradox. This has grown from the modern world celebrated by Baudelaire, the dynamic life of the Parisian streets, and inevitably it has developed the modern poetics of collage and disjunction. As Marshall McLuhan pointed out in the 1960s, nothing is so bizarre as the juxtapositions that occur everyday on the front page of a newspaper, and television has subjected the post-modern sensibility to even greater incongruity. A popular film which exploits this is *The Gods Must Be Crazy*. This tells various stories, in parallel, of a Kalahari bushman, a Marxist guerrilla *à la Castro*, a love-sick backwoodsman, and a pretty city teacher lost in the outback, and it manages to interweave these discontinuous worlds into a lyrical whole. Federico Fellini often turns the mad competition of opposite tastes into a melancholic spectacle of hilarious sadness. Nearly every one of his movies has a scene, a post-modern carnival, where the media force young and old, priests, entertainers and sensualists, into frantic confrontation. The social lines are crossed, everyone comes out confused and exhausted. This kaleidoscopic carnival is not to everyone's taste, and it certainly can be tiresome; but it is normal enough in the global village to deserve continual representation. Thus many artists such as Rauschenberg and Kitaj and architects such as Stirling and Gehry make an art of incongruity. If so much of everyday life is heterodox, the best artists will deal with this reality.

From Exclusion to Inclusion

Another shift in the post-modern world is towards openness, tolerance, inclusion. It is not just the taste for heterogeneity which has brought this about, but also the new assertions of minority rights, of 'otherness' as a predominant, even desirable, category. Now groups like to position themselves on the periphery – 'ex-centrics' as these self-styled outcasts are called. The women's movement is characteristic of many post-modern movements that were taken up in the 1960s to become accepted political forces in the 1970s. No single movement is typical of the new agenda politics, the pluralism of groupuscles. If the world village has created the consciousness that everyone belongs to an interdependent minority, then this results in a certain *realpolitik*. There is a grudging tolerance of difference, in the inner cities a 'live and let live' (as long as the jobs do not run out). Also, in the West, there is a more cosmopolitan attitude towards conflicting world views. The ideology of Modernism was exclusivist at its core, seeking to draw into one sensibility, and view of history, the plurality of discontinuous cultures. The modern project was the emancipation of humanity conceived (without understanding the fact) as a white, European, rationalist male. Its characteristic creations were the factory, Sixth Avenue in New York, the Museum of Modern Art, the Ford Motor Company, the straight line history of Modern Art from Impressionism to Abstract Expressionism, the philosophies of pragmatism, nihilism and Logical Positivism and, above all, the emphasis on steady economic growth at all costs. Ultimately, Modernism is the ideology of modernisation, and it lasted as long as that Faustian goal could be pursued seriously by the best minds.

After the 1960s people became aware of the 'limits of growth', of the social upheavals caused by modernisation, and conscious that they would only increase as modernisation was exported to the Second, Third and Fourth Worlds. If it is not the destruction of the ozone layer, it will be the creation of three more megalopoli of thirty million people; if it is not limited nuclear war between two countries, it will be the coercion of their populations into factories to work for the richer nations. The First World has sent its industrialisation packing to Mexico City and South Korea, and tried to keep the monopoly of the control technologies, the information industries, to itself. Yet one of the benevolent paradoxes of the post-modern situation is that it willingly includes the modern and pre-modern conditions as essential parts of its existence. It does not take an aggressive stance with respect to an agricultural civilisation; it has not sought to destroy indust-rialisation, nor put forward a single totalising ideology. The post-modern sensibility thrives on dispositions different from its own, and recognises that life would be horribly diminished if it all took place in the global city. In fact it has rediscovered an old truth; meaning consists precisely (if only partly) in difference. Opposition creates significance in the arts, in ideas, styles and life. Oppositions are absolutely necessary for establishing identity. Even the marketplace turns this philosophy into a slogan: 'what sells is the difference that makes a difference'.

This enjoyment of difference helps explain why the content of so much Post-Modernism is the past seen with irony or displacement. It is the realisation that we can return to a previous era and technology, at the price of finding it slightly different. The post-modern situation cultivates a sensibility that is a compound of previous ones, a palimpsest, just as the information world depends on technologies and energies quite different from its own. The present situation not only includes the previous ones, but benefits from them. We now have the luxury of inhabiting successive worlds as we tire of each one's qualities, a luxury which previous ages with their lack of opportunity did not have. There is no dictatorship of the cognitariat, nor is there an exclusive aristocracy or bourgeoisie, but rather the first paraclass to have it all ways.

[45] **Gae Aulenti and ACT, Musée d'Orsay Conversion**, 1980-6. *An inclusive architecture and view of the past and present which accepts contrary values and makes a varied comment on them. Nineteenth-century tastes in art, both academic and modern, are mirrored by twentieth-century ironies and technology, as well as beautiful lighting and a very rich development of layered space. (C Jencks)*

THE POST-NATIONAL WORLD:
THINKING WILD THOUGHTS

Reflecting on the present, one cannot help thinking of twentieth-century catastrophes which were indirectly caused by modernity: two World Wars, (when mechanised killing resulted in one hundred million deaths), the Holocaust and Stalin's liquidation of some thirty million people. Inevitable in this account of recent disasters is the Hiroshima bomb, and the genocide in Vietnam and Cambodia. Whatever one thinks of the morality of these acts, their scale is modern; their magnitude is only possible after the break-throughs of modernisation – Fordist centralisation and mass production. Furthermore, as Zygmunt Bauman has argued in *Modernity and the Holocaust*, it is the mind-set of modernity with its instrumental reason and pragmatism, which are also indirect but important causes of mass-killing. Where efficiency, cost-benefit-analysis and functionalism become the dominant values of a culture, there genocide is possible.[62]

Jean-François Lyotard goes so far as to claim that the Holocaust has 'refuted' the modern project, the emancipation of humanity. He calls this the 'Auschwitz' refutation:

> I would argue that the project of modernity (the realisation of universality) has not been forsaken or forgotten but destroyed, 'liquidated'. There are several modes of destruction, several names which are symbols for them. 'Auschwitz' can be taken as a paradigmatic name for the tragic 'incompletion' of modernity . . . At 'Auschwitz', a modern sovereign, a whole people was physically destroyed . . . It is a crime opening postmodernity . . . [63]

This is not the only 'crime opening postmodernity'. Today, scientists who have studied biodiversity say that we are entering the sixth major period of mass-extinction. Because habitats are being destroyed by modernisation some twenty-seven thousand species are lost per year; that is, one hundred a day, three an hour.[64] This latest era of mass extinction is caused not by external forces but, for the first time, by a single species – human beings.

Consciousness of this is something new and it leads to what could be called 'wild thought'; thinking about the unthinkable, discussing cosmic tragedies as if they were happening elsewhere, on another planet and to non-humans. Such dispassionate thought about catastrophe is a prevalent mode today. The daily newspaper is likely to recount a slaughter in Somalia or Bosnia with all the matter-of-factness of a stock report.

In considering what is likely to occur in the post-national world and its possible form of future governance, we are led to predict trends already underway, along with conceivable tragedies. Nations and nationalism were

62 Zygmunt Bauman, *Modernity and the Holocaust*, Polity Press, (Cambridge), 1989.

63 Jean-François Lyotard, *The Postmodern Explained to Children, Correspondence 1982-1985*, Turnaround (London), 1992, pp30-1, 40, 91.

64 Professor EO Wilson has studied the various studies on extinction and come up with these figures in *The Diversity of Life*, Allen Lane (London), 1993, p280.

two quintessential creations of the modern world, and we can predict that these modern formations will change under extreme pressure. It is obvious, from the inaction over aggression in the Bosnian experience, that nations, like individuals, do not act until they have to, until just before or after an enormous catastrophe. This is not only because they are confused, and committed to the *status quo*, but because all institutions are enmeshed with others and it takes a sudden force from outside to break these chains. Just as a sudden thaw breaks an ice-flow, just as a downpour breaks a log-jam, so we may find that a world calamity creates a new stage of world government.

Today there are several incommensurable trends leading towards global interconnection and world government. On the ambivalent side there are the three hundred and fifty largest multinational companies controlling an extraordinary one-third of all world trade. That is what makes the system global. Potentially positive global forces are the exponential growth in communications and the world information network; even the spread of English as a second language to one-sixth of the world, although the French and Chinese might think otherwise. On the obviously negative side, there are ecological catastrophes such as runaway pollution.

Two political trends are highly significant. The first is the spread of

[46] **Freedom House Map of World Democracy**. *The Map of Freedom is based on a survey which analyses the degree to which fair and competitive elections occur, individual and group freedoms are guaranteed and press freedoms exist. (Courtesy of Freedom House, New York)*

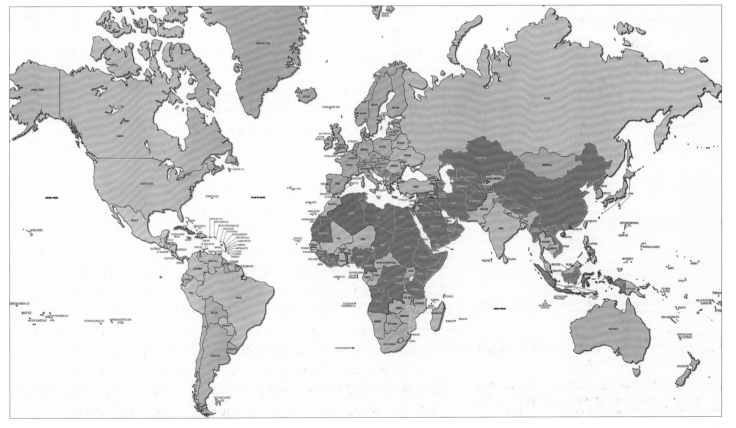

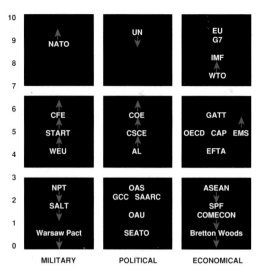

	MILITARY	POLITICAL	ECONOMICAL
10			EU
9	NATO ↑	UN ↓	G7
8			IMF
7			WTO
6	CFE ↑	COE ↑	GATT ↑
5	START	CSCE	OECD CAP EMS
4	WEU	AL	EFTA
3	NPT ↓	OAS GCC SAARC	ASEAN
2	SALT ↓	OAU	SPF COMECON
1	Warsaw Pact ↓	SEATO ↓	Bretton Woods ↓
0			

GLOSSARY OF TERMS

NATO - North Atlantic Treaty Organisation
UN - United Nations
EU - European Union
G7 - Group of Seven
IMF - International Monetary Fund
CFE - Conventional Forces Europe
START - Strategic Arms Reduction Talks
WEU - Western European Union
COE - Council of Europe
CSCE - Conference on Security and Co-operation in Europe
AL - Arab League
OECD - Organisation for Economic Co-operation and Development
CAP - Common Agricultural Policy
EMS - European Monetary System

EFTA - European Free Trade Area
GATT - General Agreement on Tariffs and Trade
WTO - World Trade Organisation
NPT - Nuclear Non-proliferation Treaty
SALT - Strategic Arms Limitation Talks
OAS - Organisation of American States
GCC - Gulf Co-operation Council
SAARC - South East Asian Treaty Organisation
ASEAN - Association of South East Asian Nations
SPF - South Pacific Forum
COMECON - Council for Mutual Economic Assistance

[47] **Transnational organisations** – *their relative power on a scale of ten and their recent rise and decline. Two and a half thousand such organisations have been created since 1945, a binding network which often keeps nations from aggression.*

65 Freedom House Surveys are made annually. For the 100 year comparisons *see* Gregory Fossedal, *The Democratic Imperative – Exporting the American Revolution*, Basic Books (New York), 1989, p16.

democracy. Democratisation, as measured by free elections, human rights, relatively free press, etc, has become more common in the last hundred years (especially a trend of the 1970s which was reversed only in 1992). In 1880 less than one-third of the world was democratic whereas today, in a general sense which the institute Freedom House has defined, almost 60 per cent is democratic or quasi-democratic.[65] Secondly, transnational organisations, such as NATO, have become more empowered. Since World War II some two and a half thousand of these have come into being. Bodies such as the UN, ASEAN, IMF, OAU, GATT and AL have begun to make nations think twice about starting wars. Such institutional and financial networks have ensnared the nation-state within a web of commitments inhibiting, if not altogether stopping, aggression. Moreover, as writers have noted since Immanuel Kant, democracies tend neither to be aggressive nor to start wars. Most importantly, there has been a proliferation of non-government organisations, NGOs, committed to peace and a sustainable ecology – Amnesty International and Oxfam to name but two. Greenpeace's prevention of the multinational Shell Oil Company dumping its used oil platform in the Atlantic ocean, 1995, shows the kind of international activism possible. The ecological merits of the case may be arguable, but there is no doubt that Greenpeace was successful in mustering support in several nations and bringing this to bear on the boardroom floor, of both the British government and Shell. The NGOs, as a whole, are creating an emergent tradition of global citizenship, a supranational consciousness and language.

These several trends taken together, in addition to the outbreak of regional ethnic wars (forty-five underway in the nineties), have led some theorists to see an empowered United Nations as a future possibility or, perhaps, the creation of an entirely new, more effective, world institution. If historical precedent is anything to go by, and we are heading towards global governance, then its character will also be determined by the specific events which bring it into being. The particular system of power dominant today – regional 'spheres of influence' led by the USA and UN – was locked-in by World War Two and the Cold War.

What kind of events might create the mandate for an effective world government? A runaway greenhouse effect, which many scientists are predicting; or perhaps a cometary collision, which a few think likely. The destruction of world resources which is now underway – such as the diminishing stocks of wheat and fish – could legitimise an international body and give it the power to control nations. In late 1995 the United Nations finally got the nations of the world to agree for the first time on a treaty to regulate fishing in the high seas. Whether this will stop the catastrophic over-fishing remains to be seen. It is not hard to imagine other legitimising catastrophes such as a limited nuclear exchange started by accident. The contestants, as well as the rest of the world, might then suddenly focus their collective mind on creating an impartial super-force. Today, there are eleven declared nuclear powers and many are resuming testing. By the year 2000 there are likely to be twenty, and that means the chances of an accidental exchange will go up exponentially.

A nagging question is whether anything less than such a tragedy is sufficient to break what is so clearly inadequate and immoral: the *status quo* of oligarchic control by powerful sovereign states and superpowers messing around in places such as Bosnia so as to ensure the slow strangulation of a nascent country. Yet, could these cynical powers sometimes be preferable to an insensitive leviathan? Many Europeans, such as Isaiah Berlin, argue that the bureaucracy and arbitrariness of a world government would be infuriating and actually cause civil wars. The argument is that an empowered UN would act slowly, sluggishly and insensitively, enraging all the contesting parties. Following this note, one might say, to paraphrase EM Forster, 'Two cheers for Global Democracy; two are quite enough'. The battle over the EU and its possible federal power is a dress rehearsal for an impending world government, and we can learn something from both sides of this debate about the importance of integrated government and the necessity of resisting central power. Concepts such as subsidiarity, regionalism, checks and balances, heterarchical and rotating power might be given more substance as we are pushed towards the ultimate leviathan. Here, underground traditions of democratic thought and experiment are important. Some of this is well codified in existing laws and literatures; the spirit of 1776 and utopian literature. Some of it is emergent from existing, grass-roots traditions; participatory democracy organised on Internet, the NGOs and what Richard Falk calls 'citizen pilgrims'.[66] We can see here a type of globalisation from below countering that pushing forward from above – the three hundred and fifty multinationals. These bottom-upwards traditions could have a profound effect in shaping the emergent institutions, just as they did at the beginning of the American Revolution. The freedom we have to shape events, born in catastrophe at the creative edge between order and chaos, is limited, but real. As Louis Pasteur said, 'fortune favours the prepared mind'. Benign outcomes of catastrophe favour prepared institutions. As the American Revolution showed, underground streams can suddenly be pushed to the top and by doing so create a river rushing in a more favourable direction.

[48] **Greenpeace** defeated a multi-national, Shell, and a nation, the UK. (Greenpeace and SIMS)

66 Richard Falk, Professor of International Law at Princeton, has invented this concept and discussed it at the Portrack Seminars; *see* note 13, p19.

If some world governance is indeed approaching, we might accentuate the type we want before it is thrust upon us, and nurture the constituency which will keep it true to the principle of powers balanced between nations and supranational bodies, NGOs and local governments. The idea of post-modern liberalism is to keep the valid aspects of modern universalism while acknowledging the truths of emergent multiculturalism.[67] I believe any policy which is not balanced carefully on this dilemma will fail to meet the potential of our unique situation.

The view of history I am assuming here is post-modern in the sense that it lays stress equally on volition and accident; the ideals of people and contingent events, human goals and the process by which one achieves, or misses, them. The post-national world hardly means the disappearance of nations, but rather the end of their dominance and the rise of multiple alternatives including an effective (or malevolent) super-state.

POST-SOCIALISM AND SOCITALISM

My list of seventy posts (pages 14-15) reveals some of the important shifts underway today, but by no means all. One of the most momentous is post-socialism: the slide of centralising doctrines – Marxism, socialism and communism – into something else, and the social realignment of, perhaps, one third of humanity. If ever the label 'post' were apposite, it is in these slight, determinant glides away from an established position. 'Economies in transition', as former socialist states are now called, are clearly leaving a central planning tradition while still keeping some attachments to this past, as they set out for different destinations that are still not clear.

These transient economies slide, glide, fall, jump, or even stall – to where? Poland, the Czech Republic, Hungary, Slovakia, the former East Germany, Slovenia, Croatia appear to have reached a dynamic 'socitalism', that is, socialised capitalism. Russia, Romania, Bosnia and Albania are caught somewhere between systems in stagnant indecision – failing states and economies verging on anarchy. But a great paradox has emerged. Those states that have successfully gone capitalist – responding to administered bursts of 'shock therapy' via reintroduced market forces – have re-elected Neo-Communist bosses! This is true in 1995 in Poland, Hungary, Lithuania and Bulgaria. Here are pm-fuzzy logic and U-turns and hybridisation on a national scale. Socitalism indeed! One reason for this hybridisation is pragmatic: the old communist bosses and parties know how to get things done, and many of these leaders have enriched themselves and grabbed the instruments of power, both economic and political. The question is, can these former communists really make the new socitalism

67 Such post-modern liberalism is the keynote of my *Heteropolis: Los Angeles, The Riots and the Strange Beauty of Hetero-Architecture*, Academy Editions (London/New York), 1993.

work? As with Western versions of radically mixed economies, the answers will no doubt vary.

For the moment, parts of Eastern Europe have effectively been turned into neutral zones, or 'Austrianised'. Indistinct partnerships with NATO are encouraged by the West and discouraged by Russia, and thus we have a corresponding 'states in transition' model for this bloc. They lean to the West, but not so far as to provoke the Russian bear; they anticipate joining the European Union, the EU, but only by the year 2002. Here, sliding and gliding is very directed.

Who can figure out what the unstable hybrid in China should be called? Cowboy capitalism/state socialism? Finally, as with other post-modern discourses, it appears that no field is distinct from another, and the outcome of social/economic/political questions is resolved because of differences in culture. How will a formerly Confucian culture cope with rampant corruption, mass labour migration, world communication and ecological melt-down? They will have to invent new Chinese institutions and languages to meet these challenges. Already their version of cowboy capitalism/state socialism is unique and, while the leaders say they want to imitate Singapore, the business community in Shanghai is actually closer to Hong Kong.

Whatever the future hybrid, the short-lived student movement in China shows some of the characteristic changes in style brought about by an attempt to merge opposite systems. Motivated by a minority appeal for social justice and increased freedom, the events of Tiananmen Square were essentially spontaneous and self-organising, dependent on decentralising technologies such as the fax, two-way radio, motorbike, television and telephone. These allowed instant local and global communication. The style and content were quintessentially hybrid, mixing quotes from Mao with phrases taken from the French and American Revolutions and their Bills of Rights. Indeed, its symbol, the Goddess of Democracy, was a mixture of French *Liberté* and the American *Statue of Liberty*, and was erected across from the large portrait of Mao in Tiananmen Square. The music during the long hours of waiting varied from Chinese songs to broadcasting, on makeshift loudspeakers, the 'Ode to Joy' from Beethoven's Ninth Symphony – a message of global brotherhood.

Whenever an international television crew swung its cameras over the crowds, up went the two-finger salute of Winston Churchill. (Did it have some specific Chinese overtone beyond 'V for Victory'?) Headbands had dual language slogans – 'Glasnost' above its Chinese translation (again so television could beam the message both to China and the English-speaking world). When the final debacle came, its global impact was

[49] **Tiananmen Square**, *4 June 1989, as seen on French television and by the rest of the world.* (C Jencks)

immediate because of television, and it even had some influence on the vote for democracy that was taking place in Poland at the time. Just after the students were crushed, on 4 June 1989, Solidarity won an extraordinary landslide victory that neither they nor the Polish Communist Party had foreseen – all one hundred and sixty-one seats that were open to it in the lower house, the Sejm, and ninety-nine out of a hundred seats in the upper house, the Senate. In twenty-four hours the Dictatorship of the Proletariat had taken a Leninist two-step, one back, one forward. Never had political events in these parts of the world been seen, communicated, analysed and judged so quickly by the globe. Furthermore, this quick reaction of the information world had a feedback effect on the events themselves – for the most part positive.

This example of world communication and hybridisation may be opposed by the politicians but, ironically, they are also going through a comparable transformation as they continue to introduce market forces and such things as openness and legality in banking (both of which have a way to go). Their selective introduction of the fax, Internet and television has further hybridised their culture. Many communist leaders have, along with their families, become very rich – 'communism for the masses, hidden capitalism for the classes'? This would not be the first time that such hypocrisy has become institutionalised; but it is unstable because it lacks legitimacy.

The idea of 'post-socialism' has been in the air in Britain since the early eighties and, given this relatively short time-span, it will probably take another ten years or so before we understand what the concept entails. For the right it means the end of the nanny state, if not the entire Welfare State. Yet under Margaret Thatcher's eleven years of market rhetoric state spending as a percentage of GNP only declined from 43 to 38 per cent – before rising back up to 40 per cent. The many entitlements in the system, an aging population and a host of other commitments have meant that, whatever anyone says, the leviathan rolls on and gobbles up people's money. The same is true in the USA, where Military Keynesianism takes some of the place of welfare; state spending as a percentage of GNP, in spite of the 'peace dividend', is getting higher (and the dividend never happened).

In effect, populations in the West are crypto-socialists of varying kinds. They want as many entitlements, rights, health services, roads, defence expenditures and educational supports as they can possibly squeeze out of the system without it either going broke or coercing them. Like the Chinese leaders, they want to square the circle. That is why so-called capitalist systems are also tending towards radical hybridisation, socialism.

To reiterate in general terms, it is an economy divided equally between [50] state spending, Fordist and Post-Fordist enterprise. There is no magic to this three-way equal split, but if state spending rises well over 40 per cent of GNP, there will be long term problems and, if the 'free market' part of the economy shrinks below 30 per cent, it will not generate enough invention and growth to pay for the state. These are the rough bands in which socialism works.

More debatable are the cultural and public goals which unify a polity. Here, modernist systems of capitalism and socialism have proved inadequate; and post-modernising systems of consumer society and socitalism are not much better. Socialism has always had a small moral and cultural component – the idealism of community, the spirituality of Ruskin and Morris – but these have always been marginalised in practice; capitalism has always had a small place for the widely touted ideals of personal freedom and growth, but in practice has made them subordinate to large corporate and national growth. Communitarianism, cultural conservation and the social market, which are all catchwords of the nineties, are worthy if unexceptional goals of the state. But it is clear, in the First World at any rate, that the state cannot supply morality and spiritual direction. These have to be grown up from the bottom in conversation with a top which is slightly elevated above the state; that is, the universe.

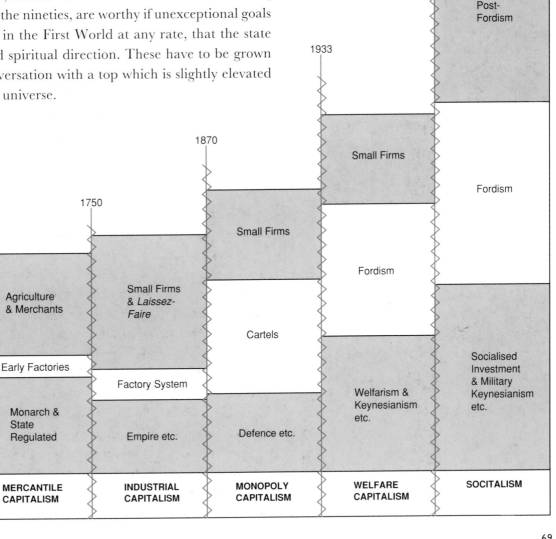

[50] **Five stages of economic growth**. *This ideal type model, generalising growth in the First World, accentuates the stages by representing a gradual process as discrete jumps. The dramatic increase in the Post-Fordist sector and the throroughly mixed economy of Socialism – a three-way equal split – are transformations of earlier structures. Each new stage of capitalism is brought in by a crisis, indicated by red zig-zags, which leads to restructuring.*

[51] **Model of the Universe** conceived as expanding from a common origin, first through inflation and then as a series of jumps.

A NEW METANARRATIVE?

As the year 2000 and a global civilisation approach, the inadequacies of traditional and modern cultures become more apparent. Yet it is also clear that there is no future which does not relate fundamentally to the past. Christianity, Islam and Hinduism may be, as are other religions, only partial spiritual traditions. However, the era of creating new vital religions is over and it was so more than a thousand years ago. We cannot return to the magical state of mind. Furthermore, modernist substitutes for religion – the metanarratives of social emancipation, progress, universal brotherhood, nature as norm – have also gone the way of traditional religions. They have some relevance, but are not completely adequate goals towards which public, spiritual and artistic life can be constantly focused.

An incredulity towards metanarratives is Lyotard's definition of the postmodern. To exaggerate, as he does, Auschwitz refutes the idea of universal history and progress, just as the Salman Rushdie Affair refutes the idea of universal Islam; and the Christian inaction in Bosnia refutes its own notion of the universal brotherhood of mankind. Who can believe that the State, or humanity in general, or any historic religion is a worthy focus for belief? Obviously a lot of people do, but not very deeply.

Weak belief has strong causes. People go on worshipping in traditional ways, but at the same time *à la carte*, selectively, with half their heart and head. The Church insists that this is wrong; a good Catholic must take the whole menu. But then it too wanders off, engaging selectively in *liaisons dangereuses* with Islam or Chinese communists to reaffirm the traditional role of women; or it bargains *à la carte* with repressive regimes in South America to reaffirm the traditional power of men. Cheating, of course, has always gone on, and a church founded on original sin has quite a good record to keep up in this department. Yet, if one looks at the scale of the practice, there has never before been an era in which masses of leaders and followers both cheat. Here again is a consequence of weak belief in the institutions we create.

Is a strong belief in anything possible today? Is there any focus suitable for art, culture and the public realm – something to which we can dedicate our lives and spare time? One answer, suggested by Thomas Berry and Brian Swimme, is that *The Universe Story* (the title of their 1992 book) is a possible, unifying focus.[68] We have only recently understood much of this story from science and history, and these two authors try to recount it from the beginning, fifteen billion years ago, as a single, unbroken narrative.

68 Brian Swimme and Thomas Berry, *The Universe Story, From the Primordial Flaring Forth to the Ecozoic Era*, Harper (San Francisco), 1992.

The idea that the story of the universe could be a new credible metanarrative is an interesting one. It certainly would replace humanism – man the measure of all things – with the larger picture in which the cosmos is the measure of all things. It could possibly give direction, orientation and meaning to human activity, but not result in a reductive anthropocentricism.

Because of physical laws such as gravity, and the tendency for them to make all matter and life self-organise, the universe shows ever-increasing organisation. For instance, stars and planets inevitably evolve out of gas and exhibit a kind of teleology, or purposeful growth, in this direction. Self-organising, material evolution along well-defined pathways precedes organic evolution, and operates according to different laws than natural selection. It could be called crystallised or focused evolution; the tendency of all material systems to develop towards greater complexity.

Organic evolution also has a general direction towards greater complexity; it is not only propelled by these same self-organising forces but also by natural selection. If we present this progress (a concept biologists dislike because of its anthropocentrism) with a visual metaphor, it would *not* be the usual Darwinian evolutionary tree, which is much too pleasant, but an over-pruned bush. As Stephen Jay Gould argues, in *Wonderful Life*, nature is a very grim reaper, and natural selection means what he calls natural 'decimation' – killing off nine so that the best tenth might survive. The two types of evolution – crystallised and natural – do combine to produce more highly organised systems and individuals, which is the main plot of the universe story, but it is a progressive drama with many setbacks.

If we adopt another metaphor, and chart the last six hundred and fifty million years as a whole, we find an increasing slope of progress; that is, an increasing number of species, genera, families and biomass – all good news – but also terrible punctuations and awful suffering. There is the Permian/Triassic transition, when perhaps 92 per cent of all species were wiped out; or the most recent one, sixty-five million years ago, when 76 per cent of the species became extinct. The story depends on the focus: the slope and jumps are positive, the catastrophes negative and the overall graph perhaps tragic, but nonetheless optimistic.

At all events the universe story is one of increasing complexity – complexity theory is one of its leading foundations – and evolution towards ever-increasing feeling, sensitivity, mental power and organisation. It contends that we are fundamentally built into the laws of the universe, but are not necessarily its final achievement; *At Home in the Universe*, as the Complexitist Stuart Kauffman's book is titled, 'without being master of the universe'.

Berry regards science as the longest unbroken meditation on the universe,

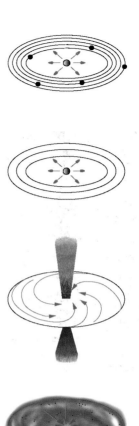

[52] **Crystallised Evolution**. *The tendency of all matter to self-organise because of the four fundamental forces is evident in the birth of stars and planets. This five-stage self-organisation was theorised more than twenty years ago, but only confirmed by the Hubble Space Telescope in May 1995. Stage one shows clouds of gas and dust pulled together by gravity – which is clearly shown in stage two. Gravity, along with other forces, causes rotation – the third stage – which results in jets of gas shooting out from the centre. When the star becomes massive enough to shine – stage four – the jets shut off, the star stops spinning and the disk condenses to form planets, stage five. This is natural, directed evolution without natural selection.*

[53] The General Trend of Organic Evolution
appears to be positive if we concentrate on the envelope curve connecting all the smaller curves. However, five major mass extinctions, which wiped out 70 to 92 per cent of all species, raises a question about the inevitable progress in species and biomass. The last extinction, sixty-five million years ago, destroyed the ammonids and dinosaurs and allowed mammals, including us, to flourish. We appear to be at the start of the sixth mass extinction, when one-tenth of all species has already been cut back because we are inadvertently destroying habitats. Even though these mass extinctions occur, the sun is beneficently pouring in more free energy, and thereby indirectly creating more biomass. Hence the assumption of an ascending envelope curve that reaches higher and higher ceilings: these would be the carrying capacity of earth at different epochs.

Admittedly, much in this diagram is based on hypotheses and limited paleontological evidence, but at the present time it seems a good bet. The implications are positive: other things being normal – with no cometary impacts, or nasty species like us – life on planets will ordinarily diversify and flourish. There is a general, if not inevitable, direction to organic evolution. (Sources: Evolutionary Progress, edited by Matthew Nitecki, University of Chicago (Chicago), 1988, pp42, 300; Rick Gore, 'The March Toward Extinction', National Geographic, June 1989, pp662-99.)

and it is true that science tells a coherent if not entirely consistent story. Inevitably, because scientists are trained in scepticism and dispute, they may not see the narrative or its import, nor understand the basically spiritual message they are bringing. Why is it spiritual? Because the universe is a single, unbroken, creative event which is still unfolding with human beings as essential parts of its story; because it inevitably produces surprising, humorous creations of beauty; because its laws are mysteriously complex and finely tuned; because it is so enjoyable and because there is strong evidence that, given enough time, it must produce culture.

The universe story is also a secular narrative of power, accident, entropy and 'just one crazy thing after another'. Chaos, anarchy and dissolution are just as essential to the drama as increasing organisation, and there is no final certitude that a benign state will prevail. Nevertheless, given enough time, it is inevitable that nature must produce culture; sentient creatures that feel first, then think and develop aesthetic and spiritual traditions. Of course some scientists dispute this, and think life and higher organisation are accidental and one-off. They argue that if you could run the universe story again and again it would always show radically different outcomes, some with no life. There is indeed an irreducible accidental aspect to history (Einstein was wrong; God does play dice) but there are also laws of emergence which virtually guarantee increasing organisation. The work of the Nobel laureate Ilya Prigogine and his book *Order Out of Chaos* typifies the argument which is coming increasingly from many quarters; the complexity scientists at the Santa Fe Institute, those who support the cosmological anthropic principle, scientists such as Freeman Dyson, Paul

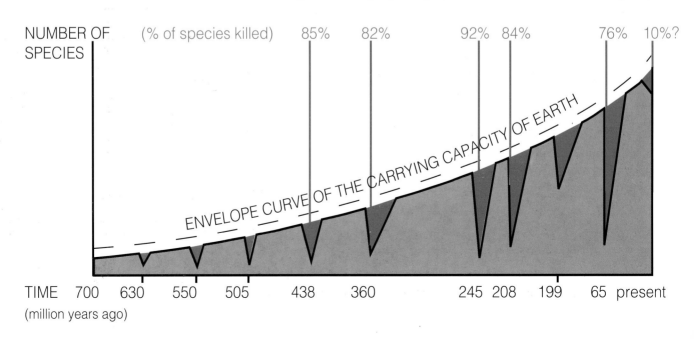

NUMBER OF SPECIES (% of species killed) 85% 82% 92% 84% 76% 10%?

ENVELOPE CURVE OF THE CARRYING CAPACITY OF EARTH

TIME 700 630 550 505 438 360 245 208 199 65 present
(million years ago)

Davies and Fred Hoyle and evolutionists such as Allan Wilson.[69]

The last mentioned shows that there is a 'cultural drive' in nature and, the bigger the brain size to body size of a species, the stronger this drive, the faster it goes. Birds, dolphins, chimpanzees have large brain to body size ratios, and their evolution has been concomitantly faster. We have seen how, with the arrival of the information world, our cultural evolution has accelerated. When one watches attempts to teach chimpanzees to speak – using computers because, of course, they do not have a larynx – one sees how they can master complex sentences and thoughts. For instance, they can respond to the verbal command: 'go get the ball outdoors and put it in the refrigerator'. This bizarre sentence, which they have never before heard, demands that they distinguish the ball outside (which they do not see) from the one inside the room (which they do). That takes quite a lot of thought and will power because the first temptation, even for children, is to get the ball one sees. In addition, chimpanzees reveal rudimentary tool-making skills and general creativity in other ways; they are also part of a society and primitive culture where ideas and habits are passed on. In short, they learn and create. Scientists at the Santa Fe Institute of Complexity call all living creatures 'complex adaptive systems', CAS, because of this basic truth.[70] The universe creates complex adaptive systems – that is, living creatures like us – which are always trying to figure out what the universe is. This spiritual quest is normal, inevitable, and will always emerge in evolution. Much twentieth-century modern philosophy – that of Heidegger, Wittgenstein, Sartre and Derrida – has concentrated on the perplexity of the universe and our apparent alienation from it. Existentialists say we are forced to be free; we are thrown into a meaningless universe with no answers and we have to choose heroically between vicious alternatives on very imperfect information. They are right; we are free and this does lead to a certain anxiety of choice – indeed what is called 'overchoice' in the postmodern world. Too many alternatives. But they overrate the uncertain, the undecidable, the chaotic, and refuse to acknowledge the beautiful emergent cosmic order and our relation to it. It is time that aesthetics and the cosmic drive to learning were placed back at the centre of culture, where they belong.

It is possible that the new metanarrative can lead to this renewal. Historic religions, with their particular narratives, will have to adapt their picture of the universe and our place in it; they will have to learn a more universal morality than they now preach, an ethical system based on cosmic unfolding and dynamic balance, of justice in process, of justice as an analogue of homeorhesis (as evolutionary balance over time). If, as I am arguing, the

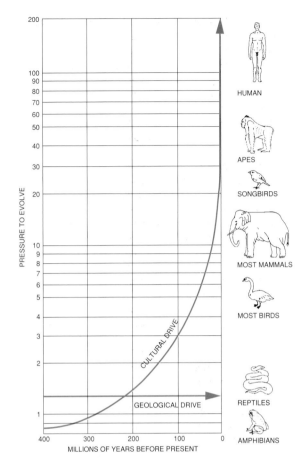

[54] The two basic evolutionary drives, external and internal to the organism, geological and cultural. As the brain to body size ratio increases the cultural drive takes over from external pressures, and evolution speeds up. Birds, mammals, songbirds and apes can learn and pass on culture, thereby adapting faster. The higher the cultural drive the faster the evolution and the stronger the pressure to evolve. Evolution is always changing its methods, forces and even laws! Today the human species – driven by late capitalism – is the natural selector writ large. Nature, having produced culture, has given way to it. (Source: Allan Wilson, 'The Molecular Basis of Evolution', Scientific American, October 1985, pp164-173.)

69 For references see my The Architecture of the Jumping Universe, Academy Editions (London/New York), 1995. The late Allan Wilson from Berekely California published some of this work in the 1980s in Scientific American.

70 For references see the previous note and, in particular, Murray Gell-Mann, The Quark and the Jaguar, Adventures in the Simple and Complex, Little Brown and Co (London), 1994.

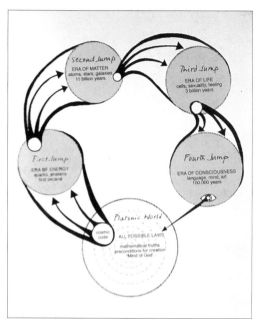

[55] **Four Jumps of the Universe**. *The most simplified narrative of the universe story comes in four main acts. After the beginning, in the first second, only energy exists – a soup of quarks and photons which expand very quickly. Then there is a sudden phase change and, for the next 11 billion years, matter unfolds into atoms, dust, gas, clouds, stars, galaxies and planets. The third jump, or emergence, is into life and the fourth is into mind, language, culture and consciousness – the eye reflecting back on the whole process. What underlies it all? The cosmic code, a selection from all possible laws. (Sources include Roger Penrose, Karl Popper, and the theory of emergence, Santa Fe Institute)*

universe really is the measure of all things, and that today we cannot not know its story, then slowly this metanarrative will gain adherents.

Take the relatively neutral questions of space, time and measurement. In traditional cultures the foot, inch and pound systems were anthropomorphic. From the Egyptian Pharoah to the King of England, dimensions were taken from the human torso. The French, being good Modernists, abstracted these units into the metre, and into measures kept under lock, key and vacuum in Paris. Since 1967, however, we have gone irreversibly cosmic as the regular decay of an atom defines time (9,192,631,770 cycles of caesium are one second); and space and weight are also measured by universal processes.

The cosmic framing of earthly processes is happening for good and bad reasons; the greenhouse effect pushes us, inevitably, to take the Gaian view of earth, and developing sciences, with their amazing discoveries, draw us into the universe story. If trends continue, such compulsions will only become stronger. Science will continue to develop and progress, unless Fundamentalists overthrow the scientific community. But let us hope we can forestall some of the worst byproducts of our consumerist growth. What I have discussed in a previous section as irreversible time, the linear emergence of novelty, looks as if it will lead us more and more towards the universe story.

What, in brief, is this story? At the simplest level it is a drama in four main acts, or jumps. In the beginning (one cannot expunge the biblical overtones) was the quantum vacuum, or plenum, the seething nothing that, [5 because of the Uncertainty Principle, allows particles to come into and go out of existence for short moments. Perhaps there was a collapse from a ten-dimensional hyperspace, perhaps the multi-space of superstrings, but, whatever happened (according to the Standard Model), there was a hot explosion and expansion. This is often mistakenly called the Big Bang. In fact it was infinitesimal, probably noiseless and heard by no one. The name was invented as a joke by Fred Hoyle, to lampoon the idea ('like a woman jumping out of a cake – too ridiculous'). But it stuck. Why? Because we live in a modernist age which wants to see and hear bangs. Such a metaphor – 'Pentagon language' as the theologian Matthew Fox calls it – alienates us from cosmic processes. Scientists are bad poets.

By contrast, Berry and Swimme call it 'the Flaring Forth', a usage I find equally problematic because of the nineteenth-century biblical overtones. Should it be called 'the ultimate mystery' – because we are never likely to understand it? I am not sure what to call this expansion and inflation but, logically speaking, I can see that there have to be laws of nature, or 'the Mind of God', or mathematical truths which make things the way they are, or whatever we want to term the preconditions for creation. This can be called the Platonic world, after Plato's idea of a transcendent realm behind the visible one. For us it consists of the cosmic code, a selection from all possible laws of those that drive our universe. It contains the laws of harmony, justice, balance, aesthetics, in so far as these human constructs have lawful behaviour; culture is based on natural principles, modes and balance, even if it partially transcends them.

In the first second after the beginning, the era of energy, the universe was a sea of quarks which expanded so fast – some say faster than the speed of light – that the balance of the four forces was finely tuned to what it is today the biggest miracle we know. The kinetic and gravitational forces were balanced so exactly – within an accuracy of one to fifty-nine (.0000000001 with fifty more zeroes in front of the 1) – that for the next fifteen billion years it neither collapsed nor blew apart. Unbelievable! If it had varied ever so slightly either way we would not be here today, nor much else.

In the next five minutes or so, the universe jumped again and went through a phase change from energy into matter. Hydrogen, the simplest atom, became the most plentiful, and its ratio to the next atom – helium – is one of the indications that the Standard Model is true. During the next eleven billion years matter evolved and formed more complex atoms, then gases, stars and clusters of galaxies. All the time the four forces – gravity, electromagnetism, the weak and strong nuclear forces – were working together and in balance to hold the universe as a universe. Over many years the heavy elements such as carbon were cooked in the heat and pressure of stars: the preconditions for life.

Life was the next big jump in organisation; nearly four billion years ago, as far as we know. Simple cells evolved, then photosynthesis allowed the earth to make better use of the sun's energy. Some six hundred million years ago, after the invention of sexual reproduction (which led to runaway variation), plants and animals evolved. Here, natural selection became much more important, and played a role alongside what I would call normal evolution: the usual tendency for all energy and matter to unfold in a directional way towards higher organisation. My last point will be strongly disputed by modernist evolutionists such as Richard Dawkins, who claim that Darwinian evolution is the standard throughout the universe and for all time. Yet such ideas fail to take into account the natural tendency for order and organisation to emerge spontaneously with no selection at all (what I have called crystallised evolution). Planets of varying size evolve naturally out of gases because of gravity and many other laws. They do not struggle for existence, compete over limited food and space, and they certainly do not have babies who are more fit. As Stuart Kauffman, and others at the Santa Fe Institute claim, there is 'order for free'; organisation emerges before natural selection operates on it.

I stress this metaphorical point because, suffering from the modernist hangover, many people including schoolchildren are still inebriated with this toxic Western brew. Metaphors matter, and if we continue to see nature as Darwinians present it – 'red in tooth and claw', or 'an arm's race', as Dawkins rephrases it – then we will continue to be alienated from it. The undeniable nasty part of nature has obscured its deeper and more beautiful qualities. Quality is the operative word: it is a consequence of the higher organisational levels that must occur over time. In the last six hundred million years nature grew its cornucopia of delights – the colours, perfumes and textures of flowers, the many sounds of birds and dolphins, the extraordinary variety of rainforests and cities. Such qualities take a long time to nurture; unimaginable eons to reach sufficient organisational depth.

Could intelligence have evolved in less than the fourteen billion years it appears to have taken? Perhaps the process is several billion years quicker, as some are now claiming, but very few scientists will believe it has not taken at least ten billion years, for such a period is necessary to create consciousness. Human consciousness is the fourth main jump in organisational depth, yet another phase change in the way things are structured. Through culture – language, institutions, science, art – consciousness reflects back on the process by which it has grown, by which it has emerged through jumps in organisation. Such knowledge about knowledge, I believe, has profound implications, and has itself emerged only recently.

The post-modern picture includes not only the universe story, but some of the theories (such as emergence) and laws (of the cosmic code) which explain it. Why should the universe hang together, and not be a pluriverse? Because of the fundamental way matter bends space and time as a tightly interrelated entity. The General Theory of Relativity shows how space and time are not the stage and procenium arch for nature – as, for instance, Kant and Newton thought – but things very much wrapped into the main action itself.

The universe is a single, creative, unfolding event whose most salient feature is sudden emergence – creativity. We now know that Newton, the Modernists and the Christians were all wrong, and that before all of them, the Egyptians and goddess cultures had a greater grasp of the truth. It is not Genesis by a male God, nor the interaction of mechanisms, but cosmogenesis. The universe is not made by a male architect, but gestates like a woman; nor is it a machine. It is a self-organising event that nurtures ever greater levels of organisation as it expands. Yet Christians and Modernists were right: we do make things, and it does look as if the universe were made – but, gestation is deeper, emergence more profound.

No doubt I am wrong in some important ways I do not understand. The lesson of emergence is that surprise, novelty, sudden jumps are always deeper than consciousness, and one step ahead of science. Nevertheless, knowledge is one-way and has deep implications. No one is going to refute gravity (in its entirety); we are not going to go back to the Ptolemaic system, or even the modern one. We cannot unlearn what we know about the universe, and this is the story of cosmogenesis: the generative nature of nature.

So the post-modern age unfolds with the post-modern sciences of complexity as a guide, setting some of the limits and possibilities for thought and action. It would be wrong, however, to say they set the entire agenda for culture, since they leave so much undecided, so much open to interpretation and creative design. We can rethink the metaphors, reinterpret the universe story and its meanings in different ways. We can get rid of the 'Big Bang' and other nasty, brutal and short appellations. We can even, when modernity is over, get rid of the label Post-Modernism – and that will be a relief. But as long as the juggernaut of modernisation asset-strips the world, the post-modern agenda will continue to flourish.

*　　　*　　　*

By way of concluding what is still an open, changing tradition, I will summarise what is necessarily a rainbow coalition of plural concerns. The post-modern agenda is an intense concern for pluralism and respect for local cultures resisting modernisation. It is the desire to cut across the different taste cultures, which now fracture society, with a new cultural strategy of double coding – mixing high and low codes, subverting the dominant from within. It is an acknowledgement of difference and otherness which those such as the feminist movement have brought to the forefront – including the re-emergence of the feminine in several discourses in which it has been suppressed, such as those concerning nature. It is the view of culture as evolutionary and support for a multiple coding that gives weight to the past, present and future. It is the understanding that knowledge is power and that, in the electronic age, information, ideas, and styles move very fast and have to be stripped of their entropic tendencies, their ersatz. It is the support for better versions of hybrid social structures – the cognitariat, socialism – than we have now. It is the continuation of the modern project of social emancipation with the agenda of multiculturalism as an equal, if opposite, logic. Finally, it is a view of the universe as the measure of all things; a single, creative unfolding event that is always trying to reach higher levels of organisation; its metanarrative the story that can orient a global civilisation.

[56] **Two Models of the Universe**. *The scientific community provides a framework for thinking about the universe, but it is up to artists, theologians and others to interpret the meaning and deep metaphors. In addition to the four jumps (previous diagram), the story can be represented in at least two other ways: as a vase or flower opening up smoothly over time (with many minor jumps represented by steps); and as an expanding sphere which unwraps from the centre. In both models the universe is held together by the four fundamental forces; both show the inflationary period at the beginning and the jumps in organisation – but the metaphors of growth are different. (Charles Jencks in association with various scientists, including Paul Davies, and sculptor Joanna Migdal).*

INDEX